W9-DDE-597

**www.booksbyboxer.com**

Published by
Books By Boxer, Leeds, LS13 4BS UK
Books by Boxer (EU), Dublin D02 P593 IRELAND
© Books By Boxer 2022
All Rights Reserved
**MADE IN CHINA**
ISBN: 9781915410047

No part of this publication may be reproduced or transmitted in any form or by any means, electronic or mechanical, including photocopying, recording or any information storage and retrieval system, or for the source of ideas without written permission from the publisher.

90's PARTY

Quiz your friends and family!

The 1990s displayed a huge shift in music trends, with genres booming, due to developments in cinema and music technology! The biggest selling single of 1990 proves that this was not going to be a normal decade of music!

First released in 1965, the Righteous Brothers' Unchained Melody experienced another wave of popularity in 1990 after being featured in the hit film Ghost, proving that Sam Wheat and a lump of clay had the whole nation feeling nostalgic! This pipped Sinead O'Connor's Nothing Compares 2 U at the top spot!

## The top 10 for 1990 in the UK was the following:

1. UNCHAINED MELODY - THE RIGHTEOUS BROTHERS
2. NOTHING COMPARES 2 U - SINEAD O'CONNOR
3. SACRIFICE/HEALING HANDS - ELTON JOHN
4. ICE ICE BABY - VANILLA ICE
5. KILLER - ADAMSKI
6. SHOW ME HEAVEN - MARIA MCKEE
7. DUB BE GOOD TO ME - BEATS INTERNATIONAL
8. VOGUE - MADONNA
9. WORLD IN MOTION - ENGLAND/NEW ORDER
10. THE POWER - SNAP!

# NINETIES IN OUR HEARTS

Why not test your knowledge of the UK charts in 1990 by answering these 5 questions. How much can you remember?

1. The two main characters in Ghost sent the whole world into a romantic mood, but can you name the actors that played Sam Wheat and Molly Jensen?

2. In the opening line of Nothing Compares 2 U, how long did Sinead O'Connor say it has been since he took his love away?

3. In Ice Ice Baby, Vanilla Ice says he is 'Killin' your brain like a poisonous _____'?

4. The music video for Madonna's Vogue was directed by an individual who later went on to direct blockbuster hits such as Seven (1995), Fight Club (1999), and Zodiac (2007). Who was it?

5. In addition to Unchained Melody, one other song from the top 10 of 1990 came from cinema – from the film Days of Thunder – which one was it?

1. Patrick Swayze and Demi Moore 2. 7 hours and 15 days 3. Mushroom 4. David Fincher 5. Maria McKee's Show Me Heaven

Some of the best shows ever created were born in the 1990s! From Buffy the Vampire Slayer and Sabrina the Teenage Witch, all the way to Friends and the Fresh Prince of Bel Air, daytime TV really began to add diversity to our screens!

Many 90s shows have since had a face lift. Sabrina, for instance, has come back to our screens, in a darker, spookier way, and the friends from Friends have gotten older and wiser.

Cartoons such as Futurama and South Park still light up our screens, with South Park still bringing new episodes out!

# 90's FOREVER

**Do you know your TV shows? Test yourself with this trivia!**

1. Which year was Charmed first aired?

2. What is the name of Sabrina's black cat?

3. Which of the friends at the end of the show Friends
wasn't in a relationship?

4. In Futurama, what 'species' is Bender?

5. Which actor plays the Fresh Prince in 'The Fresh Prince of Bel Air'?

1. 1998 2. Salem 3. Joey 4. A robot 5. Will Smith

Throughout the 90s, live music, including concerts and music festivals continued to grow globally, as more and more shows became increasingly international due to a more connected world, both through travel, broadcasting and, towards the end of the decade, the internet itself!

The 90s was a record-setting decade for many festivals we know and love. Glastonbury festival, held in Somerset, UK, had an estimated 300,000 people watching headliners, The Levellers, in 1994, making it one of their biggest ever crowds, a status that is still upheld to this day!

However, the biggest live crowd of the 1990s was in Brazil, in 1994. Copacabana Beach, on the coast of Rio de Janeiro, was home to a New Year's Eve concert performed by Rod Stewart, and had an impressive crowd of 3.5 million people!

Packed onto this world famous beach, a crowd of this size has still yet to be beaten – quite the accolade Do You Think I'm Sexy? Singer!

# 90's TRIVIA

Festivals and concerts in the 1990s were more popular than ever before, but how much do you know about some of the biggest events of the decade?

1. Now known as one of the biggest electronic music festivals in the world, due to its size and depth of line up, which UK festival launched in 1998?

2. Which Mancunian duo performed to 500,000 fans at Knebworth in 1996, with an iconic performance that was split over two nights?

3. In 1990, which artist began her 'Blonde Ambition Tour'?

4. What was the name of the Spice Girls' iconic nineties tour?

5. Hanson toured worldwide in 1998 with their tour titled 'The Albertane Tour'. What's the name of their biggest, and most iconic song?

4. The Spiceworld Tour 5. MMMbop
1. Creamfields 2. Oasis 3. Madonna

# QUEEN TRIVIA

On 24th November 1991, the world stood still as one of the most iconic musicians in UK history passed away. Freddie Mercury (born Farrokh Bulsara), was the lead singer of the world-known rock band Queen.

Mercury was diagnosed with AIDS in April 1987, but didn't make it public until his final statement, which was released after his passing. The years following the discovery, His health began to decline rapidly. With no cure in sight, there was nothing that could be done to stop this disease from spreading.

However, Freddie Mercury didn't fear his death. He pushed for his band to write more songs, so he could record them in short bursts in the studio. Freddie Mercury passed away aged 45 in his home from AIDS induced pneumonia.

## Are you a bit of a Queen fan? Why not try this trivia?

1. What year was Freddie Mercury born?

2. What was the biggest Queen song?

3. When did Queen form their band?

4. Which singer did Freddie perform the duet "Under Pressure" with?

5. Which Queen album was the first to hit number 1 in the UK?

4. David Bowie 5. A Night at the Opera
1. 1946 2. Bohemian Rhapsody 3. 1970

# 90's TRIVIA

Test your decade knowledge with these fun 90s trivia questions. Remember, all of these are pot luck, so could be about any year and any topic — let's see how much of a 90s kid you really are!

1. Who was the lead singer of 90s grunge band, The Smashing Pumpkins?

2. Family Guy premiered in 1999, but what state in the US is it set in?

3. Which band was formed first – the Backstreet Boys or NSYNC?

4. Which singer was knighted on February 4th, 1998?

5. Which action figures were described as being 'perfect for every gender'?

1. Billy Corgan 2. Rhode Island 3. Backstreet Boys 4. Sir Elton John 5. Power Rangers

We Love The
## 90's

The 90s was a dream for any budding gamer, with the release of many consoles that would revolutionise the face of gaming forever! One of the biggest releases were the Nintendo 64, released in 1996, which saw the likes of Super Mario, Banjo Kazooie, Donkey Kong and Zelda explode into the international gaming market!

The second release, and arguably biggest console release of the decade was the Sony PlayStation. Unrecognisable to its newer-generation modern counterpart, the PlayStation introduced a 'DualShock' controller, which transformed the way gaming was consumed, and is still a format that is used today! The PlayStation introduced its fans to games such as: Crash Bandicoot, Resident Evil, Castlevania, Tomb Raider and Spyro – quite the legacy!

Released towards the end of 1994, the PlayStation cost an eye-watering £299 in the UK. Whilst this amount doesn't seem much by today's standards, after inflation, this would set you back around £640, showing that the PlayStation really was a luxury for 90s kids!

Were you team PlayStation or Nintendo? What was your favourite game?

## Test your 90s gaming knowledge!

1. Who was the main villain in the Crash Bandicoot franchise?

2. In the 2001 film adaption, who played Lara Croft in Tomb Raider?

3. Which video game character is famous for running faster than their sidekick, Tails?

1. Dr. Neo Cortex 2. Angelina Jolie 3. Sonic the Hedgehog

If you were a 90s kid, you probably remember countless iconic sweets of the decade — some of which are hard to find now! Regular trips to the corner shop to get a 5p bag of sweets filled with foamy shrimps, flumps, fruit salads and flying saucers seems so far removed from the extortionate 25p Freddos of the here and now!

Kids of the 1990s loved sweets that could double up as an accessory:

Barratt's Candy Sticks, whilst unremarkable in taste, allowed kids of the 90s to pretend they were cigarette smoking rebels — for the added realism, buy these in winter to get the smoky mist on the exhale!

Additionally, candy jewellery also had kids from the 90s in a headlock. From bracelets, anklets, necklaces and rings, these were the must-have edible fashion accessory of the decade! They could also be pinged across the playground like mini slingshots — the sweet that kept on giving!

1. We have already established that Freddos are now 25p, but how much were they priced at when they relaunched in 1994?

2. Now known as Starburst, what was their name before their shock rebranding in 1998?

3. Described as 'sugar coated puffed maize and rice', these small, melty, bright, multi-coloured crunchy bites were called what?

1. 10p 2. Opal Fruits 3. Rainbow Drops

90's PARTY

Quiz your friends and family!

In 1991, the biggest selling single was the first of two UK chart toppers for Canadian Bryan Adams, with the now-classic ballad (Everything I Do) I Do It For You, clearly showing how for the first two years of the 90s, romance really was in the air!

1991 was filled with other iconic songs that remain hugely popular today! The top 10 looked like:

1. (EVERYTHING I DO) I DO IT FOR YOU - BRYAN ADAMS
2. BOHEMIAN RHAPSODY/THESE ARE THE DAYS OF OUR LIVES - QUEEN
3. THE SHOOP SHOOP SONG (IT'S IN HIS KISS) - CHER
4. I'M TOO SEXY - RIGHT SAID FRED
5. DO THE BARTMAN - THE SIMPSONS
6. ANY DREAM WILL DO - JASON DONOVAN
7. THE ONE AND ONLY - CHESNEY HAWKES
8. DIZZY - VIC REEVES & THE WONDER STUFF
9. INSANITY - OCEANIC
10. I WANNA SEX YOU UP - COLOR ME BADD

# NINETIES IN OUR HEARTS

**Why not test your knowledge of the UK charts in 1990 by answering these 5 questions. How much can you remember?**

1. Originally released in 1975, Queen's Bohemian Rhapsody opens with what 2 lines?

2. Cher's Shoop Shoop Song featured in which film, featuring Cher, Winona Ryder and Christina Ricci?

3. How many weeks did Bryan Adams stay at number one in the UK with (Everything I Do) I Do It For You?

4. Coming in at number 13, which Michael Jackson song featured the opening lyrics,

I took my baby on a Saturday bang
Boy is that girl with you?
Yes we're one and the same
Now I believe in miracles
And a miracle has happened tonight

1. Is this just real life? Is this just fantasy? 2. Mermaids
3. 16 weeks 4. Black or White

From the decade that brought us endless iconic sweets and snacks, brought over by the Americanisation of British culture, one thing stayed at the core of what it meant to be a British child in the 90s: Turkey Dinosaurs. Make your own at home!

## INGREDIENTS:

For the filling:
1 kg lean turkey mince
50 g panko breadcrumbs
1 small onion, finely chopped
1/2 tsp. garlic powder
1 tbsp. tomato ketchup
2 tsp. salt
1/2 tsp. Pepper

For the coating:
100g panko breadcrumbs
2 large eggs
100g plain flour
Salt and pepper to taste

# NINETIES IN OUR HEARTS

## Method:

1. Place your turkey mince, along with the rest of the ingredients for the filling into a bowl and mix well.

2. Roll out your filling between two layers of greaseproof paper, until the filling is around 1cm thick. Freeze for 30 minutes to make shaping the dinos easier!

3. Use dinosaur shaped cutters to cut your filling into shape. If you're feeling artistic, this can also be done freehand!

4. For the coating, place the eggs, breadcrumbs and flour in three separate bowls.

5. Dip the dinosaurs in the flour, followed by the egg and finally in the breadcrumbs.

6. Once they are all fully coated, heat oil in a pan until it is approximately 170 °C. Shallow fry for approximately 2 minutes each side, until the filling is cooked and the coating crispy!

7. Serve up with potato waffles and alphabetti spaghetti for the ultimate feast!

Name: Leonardo DiCaprio (Leonardo Wilhelm DiCaprio)
Born: 11th November 1974
Occupations: Actor, Producer, Writer
Most Famous 90s Appearance: Titanic

**Teenage heartthrob, Leonardo Dicaprio, watched his career take off to new heights in the 90s, as he went from a supporting cast member on 80s sitcom Growing Pains, to an Oscar Nominee for What's Eating Gilbert Grape in 1994 at the young age of 19, signalling his takeover of Hollywood! It wouldn't be long until his name became a household feature, but how much do you really know about this actor?**

### True or False:

1. Leonardo DiCaprio is named after Renaissance painter, Leonardo Da Vinci.

2. The Wolf of Wall Street was nominated for 92 awards in total.

3. Titanic is the highest grossing film in North America, after inflation adjustments.

4. During the 90s, DiCaprio was a member of a social squad dubbed the 'Pussy Patrol'.

5. DiCaprio first appeared on screen aged nine in children's TV show Romper Room, but was fired for being too disruptive.

4. True 5. False – he was 5 years old
3. False – After inflation, Gone With the Wind is the highest, grossing nearly $1.9 billion! Titanic comes in 5th place.
1. True 2. False – It was nominated for 133!

You can't have a brilliant movie without props, and the 90s was a very fun decade for movie props! Let's take a look at some props from popular 90s movies, and see where they are today!

### Movie: Groundhog Day
### Year: 1993

There were two working alarm clocks for this film originally, and as many as 12 non-working replicas.

Anyone who's seen the movie will know that the character Phil Connors (played by Bill Murray) destroys more than one alarm clock! So many in fact, that it is believed all versions of the alarm clock from this iconic movie had been destroyed during production.

### Movie: Jumanji
### Year: 1995

There are in fact 3 versions of the original board game prop from this wild adventure movie. With two believed to be sitting in private collections, the last is yet to be seen again. One of the two owned boards sold on eBay in 2014 for a whopping $60,800, while the other (a more user-friendly version) was sold in auction the very same year.

### Movie: Titanic
### Year: 1997

Everyone knows about the twinkling jewels of the titanic. But did you know this beautiful piece of jewellery isn't as expensive it was said to be? Made from zirconia and white gold, it's only worth $11,000, and would be worth around $425 million if this had genuine diamonds. Celine Dion's music video replica sold for $1.4 million and currently resides in Cornwall, England!

We Love The
90's

EBay may seem like a handy online tool for buying and selling today, but in 1995, it was a breakthrough website!

In 1995, Pierre Omidyar founded eBay as a hobby. That was, until his internet provider pulled him on the high website traffic, informing him that he would need to upgrade to a business account. With this cost shooting rapidly from a mere $30 a month to $250, Pierre made the decision to begin charging eBay's users.

In 1998, eBay went public, turning Pierre and his hired president Jeffery Skoll into billionaires instantly.

# 90's TRIVIA

Are you still a regular visitor to the eBay website? Let's test your knowledge now!

1. What was the first thing to be sold on eBay?

2. Which town was the first to be sold on eBay?

3. The original eBay website had a page dedicated to which deadly virus?

4. What was eBay's working name before it became the iconic eBay?

5. What was the first item sold to the UK on eBay?

1. A broken laser pointer 2. Bridgeville, California
3. Ebola 4. Auction Web 5. The Scorpions CD

Name: Cristiano Ronaldo (Cristiano Ronaldo dos Santos Aveiro)
Born: February 5th, 1985
Occupations: Professional footballer
Most Famous 90s Appearance: The 1998 World Cup semi-final

**Cristiano Ronaldo is a member of the Manchester United Football Club and also captains the Portugal National team. Growing up in Portugal, Ronaldo began playing football as a child. By age 14, he was able to play semi-professionally. He had to undergo heart surgery not too long after because of tachycardia, but recovered soon after.**

**Ronaldo now has a net worth of £367 million!**

**90's TRIVIA**

**True or false:**

1. At age 14, Ronaldo threw a chair at his teacher.

2. Cristiano doesn't have any tattoos because he often gives blood.

3. Cristiano Ronaldo is a semi-wrestler.

4. Lisbon is Ronaldo's home town.

5. Aged only 17, he scored a hat-trick on his debut.

1. True 2. True 3. True 4. False — Madeira 5. False

Again showing the influence cinema was having on the charts in the 90s, the biggest selling single of 1992 was from the film The Bodyguard. Guessed it yet?

Yes... correct! Legend Whitney Houston's iconic cover of I Will Always Love You, originally sung in 1972 by Dolly Parton, spent a whopping 10 weeks at the top of the charts!

Since its release, this legendary cover has earned the title of the best-selling song by a female artist of all time!

## The top 10 in 1992 looked like this:

1.  I WILL ALWAYS LOVE YOU - WHITNEY HOUSTON
2.  RHYTHM IS A DANCER - SNAP!
3.  WOULD I LIE TO YOU - CHARLES & EDDIE
4.  STAY - SHAKESPEARS SISTER
5.  PLEASE DON'T GO - KWS
6.  END OF THE ROAD - BOYZ II MEN
7.  ABBA-ESQUE EP - ERASURE
8.  AIN'T NO DOUBT - JIMMY NAIL
9.  HEAL THE WORLD - MICHAEL JACKSON
10. GOODNIGHT GIRL - WET WET WET

# NINETIES IN OUR HEARTS

**Think you've unlocked some memories of the 1992 charts?
Check your knowledge with the following questions:**

1. To the nearest million, approximately how many copies of I Will Always Love You have been sold?

2. Missing out on a spot in the top 10, Achy Breaky Heart was sung by which country music star?

3. The band behind Rhythm Is a Dancer, Snap!, were originally formed in which European country?

4. Please Don't Go by KWS is a re-production of a 1979 song of the same name, was released by KC and the _____ Band?

5. Erasure secured 7th spot in the end of the year's top 10 singles. What was the name of their best-selling single of all time, released in 1988?

1. 20 Million 2. Billy Ray Cyrus 3. Germany 4. Sunshine 5. A Little Respect

**90's FOREVER**

Any 1990s outfit would be incomplete without Jelly Shoes. These shiny, sometimes sparkly, and always uncomfortable sandal-style shoes were everywhere in the 90s, but where did they come from?

Made from PVC plastic, Jelly Shoes are named after the Parisian company of the same name that founded them in 1980. By mid-1980s, they began to take off in popularity, but it wasn't until the 1990s that they really blew up into mainstream fashion. After trickling down through designers and various runways of the late 1980s, by the early 90s, every kid wanted a pair of glittery plastic jelly sandals!

**Test your jelly knowledge with these quick questions:**

1. In 1998, the Coen brother's directed a film that featured a jelly-sandal-wearing-Jeff Bridges playing the role of a man mistaken for a millionaire – what was the name of the movie?

2. One particular French designer with initials 'JPG' featured Jelly Sandals on the runway – who was it?

3. The first PVC infused shoe came about earlier in the 20th century than the conception of the 'Jelly Shoe' as we know it in the 80s, but which decade was the idea first reported?

1. The Big Lebowski 2. Jean Paul Gaultier 3. 1940s

# 90's TRIVIA

The 90s was a crazy decade for new toy inventions. Technology was improving massively at this time, and children wanted more games, more creativity and overall more fun!

One of the most iconic toys of this decade was the Tamagotchi. Yes, children around the world begged their parents for this digital pet on a keychain (only to pop it into the drawer never to be seen again).

Developed in 1996 by Aki Maita and Akihiro Yokoi (from the Japanese company Bandai), the Tamagotchi has expanded from its original range, and even has video games, films and key-charms!

Bandai sold around 400,000 Tamagotchis in 1996.

## Do you know your Tamagotchi? Let's find out!

1. The name Tamagotchi is a blend of two Japanese words. Tamago, meaning 'egg', and uotchi, meaning what?

2. Aki Maita and Akihiro Yokoi won which award for their invention in 1997?

3. Using which kind of communication can two players link their Tamagotchis?

4. How many styles of Tamagotchi were originally released in 1996?

5. How long is the average Tamagotchi lifespan?

1. Watch 2. Nobel Prize 3. Infrared 4. 6 5. 12 days

## 90's TRIVIA

In 1994, the Channel Tunnel (Eurotunnel) was opened! This underwater tunnel is a unique way to travel from one country to another. At its lowest point, the tunnel reaches 75 meters below the sea bed! How crazy is that?

Engineers have been toying with the idea of an underground tunnel to cross the Channel since the early 1800s, but only began to be constructed in 1988

The Eurotunnel today transports many people to and from France and England each day, with an average of 60,000 train passengers, 4,600 trucks, and almost 7,500 cars and coaches!

### Travel Trivia!

**Have you ever travelled through the tunnel?**
**Can you guess the answers correctly?**

1. How many miles long is the Channel Tunnel?

2. How many thousand people were employed to construct the tunnel?

3. Construction began at both sides. Which side tunnelled the furthest?

4. How many tunnels are actually down there?

5. How long does it take to travel the tunnel?

1. 13.4 miles 2. 13,000 3. England 4. 3 5. 35 minutes

We Love The 90's

In the 1990s, holiday destinations abroad were more popular than any decade previous! In the modern day, places such as Dubai, Spain and Croatia are hugely popular with British tourists.

However, in the 1990s, destinations such as Turkey and Tunisia were huge contenders in the UK tourism industry!

This is largely down to the continued popularity of package holidays and resorts abroad in Europe, and all over the world!

In the 1990s, world politics shifted greatly, changing the face of worldwide travel!

The end of the Balkans war signalled an opening of tourism in Europe's Eastern Bloc, Nelson Mandela's election in 1996 led to South Africa's boom in the safari tourism industry, and gentrification in places such as Miami and L.A. meant once run-down areas of the city became hip and trendy tourist hotspots!

What was your favourite holiday you went on in the 90s?

**Travel Trivia!**

1. What year in the 1990s did the Balkans War end in Croatia, leading to a boom in tourism in the 00s?

2. How many more million people in the UK took holidays abroad in 2016, when compared to 1996?

3. Which of the following countries is now less popular with UK holidaymakers than in the nineties?

A) Germany, B) France, C) Italy

1. 1995 2. 18 million 3. B) France

# 90's TRIVIA

Test your decade knowledge with these fun 90s trivia questions.
Remember, all of these are pot luck, so could be about any year and
any topic – let's see how much of a 90s kid you really are!

1. In what year did Buckingham Palace open its
doors to the public?

2. In 1992, the first McDonalds opened in China. What city was
this in?

3. Who presented SM:TV Live with Ant and Dec?

4. What fizzy drink, popular in the 90s, had a black and white
animal on the front?

5. On which kids' show did the character Pierre Escargot appear?

1. 1993 2. Beijing 3. Cat Deeley 4. Panda Pops 5. All That

Name: Charles, Prince of Wales (Charles Philip Arthur George)
Born: November 14th, 1948
Occupations: Prince of Wales
Most Famous 90s Appearance: Assassination attempt,
Diana's death in 1997

**Prince Charles is the oldest and longest-serving heir apparent in British history. Born in Buckingham Palace, he was the first grandchild of King George VI. He married Lady Diana Spencer in 1981, whom he had two sons, William and Harry. He divorced Diana in 1996, and married Camilla Parker Bowles in 2005.**

## True or False:

1. In 1971, Prince Charles became the first heir of the Royal Family to earn a university degree.

2. He is a distant relative of 15th century nobleman Vlad Tepes (Vlad the Impaler).

3. He insists his eggs are boiled for 5 minutes.

4. He once gave Ozzy Osborne (a recovering alcoholic) a bottle of scotch as a get-well-soon gift.

5. Prince Charles is a lover of magicians.

1. True 2. True 3. False – 7 minutes 4. True 5. True

**90's TRIVIA**

A handful of chefs in the 90s had risen to stardom
(just like a nice victoria sponge cake), and brought tasteful
entertainment to mothers, fathers, grandmothers and even us 90s kids!

**Who:** Gary Rhodes
**Year:** 1994
**Show:** Rhodes About Britain

**Who:** Ainsley Harriott
**Year:** 1997
**Show:** Ainsley's Barbecue Bible

**Who:** Gordon Ramsay
**Year:** 1998
**Show:** Boiling Point

**Who:** Nigel Slater
**Year:** 1998
**Show:** Nigel Slater's Real Food Show

**Who:** Nigella Lawson
**Year:** 1999
**Show:** Nigella's Bites

### Think you know your TV chefs, why not test yourself!

1. Which TV cook-off show, which had a green and red team, did Ainsley Harriot host?

2. Which sport did Gordon Ramsey want to be a professional in?

3. What was the title of Nigella's first book?

4. What year was Nigel Slater born?

1. Ready Steady Cook 2. Football 3. How To Eat 4. 1958

90's PARTY

A TON

Quiz your friends and family!

Continuing with the hopeless romantic theme, the biggest selling single of 1993 was Meatloaf's I'd Do Anything For Love (But I Won't Do That). Described as 'Wagnerian Rock', Meatloaf's music is described as a fusion of classical operatic ballads and 20th century rock and roll, a style that is typical of the late 1980s and early 1990s!

**Meatloaf's hit beat some other strong contenders for the top spot in 1993:**

1. I'D DO ANYTHING FOR LOVE (BUT I WON'T DO THAT) - MEATLOAF
2. (I CAN'T HELP) FALLING IN LOVE WITH YOU - UB40
3. ALL THAT SHE WANTS - ACE OF BASE
4. NO LIMIT - 2 UNLIMITED
5. DREAMS - GABRIELLE
6. MR BLOBBY - MR BLOBBY
7. OH CAROLINA - SHAGGY
8. WHAT IS LOVE - HADDAWAY
9. MR VAIN - CULTURE BEAT
10. I WILL ALWAYS LOVE YOU - WHITNEY HOUSTON

**90's FOREVER**

Test your knowledge of the 1993 songs of the year, and their artists, with these 5 questions:

1. Meatloaf featured in which campy 1975 musical, as Biker Eddie?

2. Reggae and pop band UB40 were formed in which major UK city?

3. Mr Blobby first appeared on our screens in 1992 – which BBC One programme was he first premiered on?

4. Coming in at number 22 on the end of year charts, the title of 4 Non Blondes most famous song posed what question?

5. In Haddaway's What Is Love, finish the lyric: 'What is love? Baby don't _____ '

1. The Rocky Horror Picture Show 2. Birmingham 3. Noel's House Party 4. What's Up? 5. Hurt me

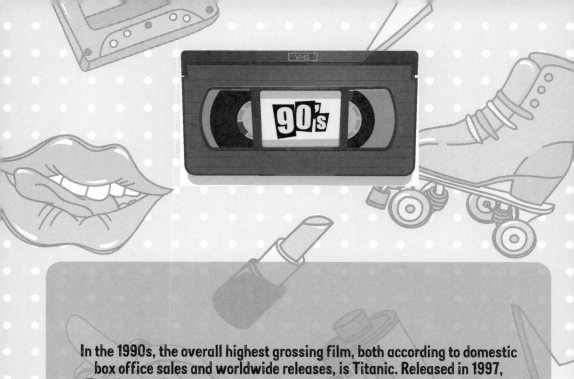

In the 1990s, the overall highest grossing film, both according to domestic box office sales and worldwide releases, is Titanic. Released in 1997, Titanic was directed by James Cameron, and starred Leonardo DiCaprio and Kate Winslet as Jack and Rose. Becoming an instant success, Titanic made an impressive $600 million on its domestic box office alone!

**The top 5 highest grossing films**
**(based on their initial box-office releases)**
**of the 1990s were:**

1. Titanic ($600 million)
2. Star Wars: Episode I - The Phantom Menace ($431 Million)
3. Jurassic Park ($357 Million)
4. Forrest Gump ($329 Million)
5. The Lion King ($312 Million)

**Do any of these surprise you? Which film do you think is most deserving of the top spot?**

# 90's FOREVER

**How much do you know about the movies that cashed it in, in the 90s?**

1. How many Academy Awards was Titanic nominated for?

2. What year was the first Jurassic Park released?

3. What is the name of the warthog from The Lion King?

4. In which US State was Forest Gump mostly set?

5. Who played Sabé in Star Wars: Episode I - The Phantom Menace?

1. 14 2. 1993 3. Pumbaa
4. Alabama 5. Kiera Knightley

## 90's FOREVER

**The 1990s really was a unique decade for adverts. With each year, they became more random and way more fun!**

Tango really hit the spot with their iconic "Orangeman" advert. Released in 1992, the advert, as you will likely remember, features a character completely in orange, running around, stopping then slapping an innocent Tango drinker. In the end, people around the world struggled to keep from slapping their pals whenever they picked up a can of tangy juice.

This advert continued until 1996, but came back to haunt our screens in the 2000s!

**Did you get tangoed? Try this true or false about the tangiest pop around!**

**1. Which year was Tango first launched?**

**2. Who owns the Tango brand currently?**

**3. Before the different flavours sold today, which flavour was Tango originally?**

**4. Tango brought out a small range of health and beauty products – hand soap and which other product?**

**5. A slush drink made from Tango became available to the public in many entertainment venues. What is this slush called?**

1. 1950 2. Britvic 3. Orange 4. Shower Gel 5. Tango Ice Blast

We Love The

90's

Colours were all the rage in the 90s. With better quality colour on TVs, brighter colours lit up our screens and eventually lit up our clothing choices too!

Blues, pinks and yellows are the three main colours attributed to the 90s, however people loved to include every bright colour to the mix. Black outlines were a must also!

Geometric shapes really took hold of fashion and household items. The 90s folk couldn't get enough of solid block triangles, circles, squares and even squiggles. Oh, and if your diary lacked hand-drawn Geometry, then were you even a 90s kid?!

# 90's TRIVIA

Test your decade knowledge with these fun 90s trivia questions.
Remember, all of these are pot luck, so could be about any year and any
topic – let's see how much of a 90s kid you really are!

1. Which video game was the first video game played in space during
the 1990s?

2. What was the most popular mobile phone of the 1990s?

3. Who famously had their ear bitten by Mike Tyson during a boxing
match in 1997?

4. What was the last Harry Potter book that was released in the 1990s?

1. Tetris 2. Starburst 3. The Nokia 3210
4. Evander Holyfield 5. Prisoner of Azkaban

## 90's TRIVIA

6. In what year did Prince Charles and Princess Diana get divorced?

7. What was the name of the popular hairstyle named after a character in a US sitcom?

8. In which year did the Channel Tunnel open?

9. Luke Perry, Jason Priestley and Shannen Doherty were the stars of which massive American teen TV drama?

10. Where did the 1992 Summer Olympics take place?

6. 1996 7. The Rachel (Friends)
8. 1994 9. 90210 10. Barcelona

The late 90s saw the release of the iconic toy... the Furby. Released in 1998, this electronic fluffy toy was created by Tiger Electronics, and took the world by storm!

Entering the market with the slogan 'Let's Have Fun', Furby resembled a hamster/owl like fluffy animal, and spoke in an invented language called 'Furbish'. Some common Furbish phrases were:

- Wee-Tah-Kah-Loo-Loo – Tell Me A Joke.

- Wee-Tah-Kah-Wee-Loo – Tell Me A Story.

- U-Nye-Ay-Tay-Doo? – Are You Hungry?

- U-Nye-Noh-Lah – Show Me A Dance.

Much like having your own furry baby, you were able to train your Furby over time to speak English, having children across the country, and the world, staring their own fur-filled families!

**Did you have your own Furby?**

# 90's TRIVIA

**Test your knowledge on these electronic fur-babies with these fun questions:**

1. To the nearest 5 million, how many Furbies were sold in the first three years of trading?

2. Approximately – to the nearest 10 – how many words could you say in Furbish?

3. In what year was the Furby last discontinued?

4. In cm, how tall were Furbies?

5. On their release, Hasbro were taken to court on the Furby's resemblance to creatures from which 80s movie?

1. 40 million 2. 100 3. A: 2018 4. 15cm 5. Gremlins

The 1990s continues to praise a solid power ballad above other genres, with Wet Wet Wet's Love Is All Around being the top selling single of '94.

As a cover of the 1968 song by English rock band, The Troggs, this cover was made for the 1994 film Four Weddings and a Funeral, again showing how cinema shaped the charts of the 90s!

## The top 10 hits of 1994 in the UK looked like this:

1. LOVE IS ALL AROUND - WET WET WET
2. SATURDAY NIGHT - WHIGFIELD
3. STAY ANOTHER DAY - EAST 17
4. BABY COME BACK - PATO BANTON
5. I SWEAR - ALL-4-ONE
6. ALWAYS - BON JOVI
7. WITHOUT YOU - MARIAH CAREY
8. CRAZY FOR YOU - LET LOOSE
9. DOOP - DOOP
10. THE SIGN - ACE OF BASE

### Do any of these surprise you?

# NINETIES IN OUR HEARTS

**Find out if your year of expertise was 1994 with these fun trivia questions!**

1. Four Weddings and a Funeral featured which dishy actor as the central character?

2. What can't Mariah Carey do, if living is without you?

3. Coming in last place on the UK top 40 for 1994, what's the title of Rednex's party anthem?

4. Who was singing about the most beautiful girl in the world in 1994?

5. What is the colour of East 17's coats from the iconic music video for Stay Another Day?

1. Hugh Grant 2. Live
3. Cotton Eye Joe 4. Prince 5. White

We Love The

# 90's

Hailed in the 90s as a City Girl's drink of choice,
largely to its appearance on Sex and the City,
the Cosmopolitan remains a staple
on any cocktail menu!

First featured on episode 2, season 2, in 1999,
this little pink drink quickly became an emblem
for all things trendy in the 90s, despite
its popularity boom late into the decade!

**90's FOREVER**

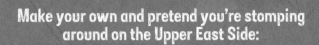

## Make your own and pretend you're stomping around on the Upper East Side:

Ingredients:
45ml lemon vodka
15ml triple sec
30ml cranberry juice
10ml lime juice
ice

## Method:

Put all the ingredients in a
cocktail shaker with ice,
and shake away - simple really!

What was your favourite
cocktail from the 90s?

We Love The

# 90's

In the 1990s, there were many televised events that were broadcast to millions and millions of people around the world! International live broadcasting continued to grow as a phenomenon in the 1990s, and as a result, the audiences for certain televised events were staggering!

The most viewed event of the 1990s was the Funeral of Princess Diana in 1997. Her sudden and tragic death sent shockwaves across the globe, and left millions of people devastated.

Her true popularity was revealed on the day of her funeral, when an estimated 2.5 billion people around the world tuned in to watch her funeral, and mourn the loss of the people's princess. Considering at the time, the world population was a little under 6 billion people, 2.5 billion is nearly half the world's population – staggering!

Another notable television broadcast of the 1990s was a concert – The Wall – that was performed at the site of the Berlin Wall, only 6 months after it was taken down. A whopping 1 billion people tuned in to this concert, which featured big name artists such as Pink Floyd, Roger Waters and Cyndi Lauper.

# 90's TRIVIA

1. What year was Princess Diana born?

2. Which 'Nothing Compares 2 U' singer also performed at the 1990 concert 'The Wall'?

3. What was Princess Diana's surname before she married?

4. To the nearest year, how many years was the Berlin Wall up for?

5. Who sang at Princess Diana's funeral?

1. 1961 2. Sinead O'Connor 3. Spencer 4. 28 years 5. Elton John

We Love The
90's

On the 11th February 1990, the world celebrated as Nelson Mandela was freed from prison in South Africa. As an anti-apartheid revolutionary, Mandela was convicted in 1964, alongside several other rebels under charges of sabotage. He served 27 years in prison, 18 of which were at a high-security, brutal prison, called Robben Island.

However, after international pressures, President F. W. de Klerk released him in 1990! After his release, Mandela went on to become a hero for South Africans, after his fight for equality and justice to bring peace to the once divided nation!

After a few years of campaigning after his release, Mandela stood for presidency in South Africa in 1994, where he became the first black president! This was a historical day in the Nation's history, and his inauguration was watched and celebrated by over 1 billion viewers globally!

He was president from the 10th May 1994 until the 16th June 1999, when he stood down. He continued his philanthropy until his death in 2013, making him one of the most loved historical figures in recent history!

**90's TRIVIA**

## Test your Nelson knowledge with some fun and interesting questions!

1. What prestigious prize was awarded to Nelson Mandela in 1993?

2. In which decade was Nelson Mandela born?

3. In which famous South African city did Mandela live?

4. How many children did Nelson Mandela have?

5. In what decade did the Apartheid in South Africa begin?

1. Nobel Peace Prize 2. 1910s 3. Johannesburg
4. 7 (6 biological, 1 step-child) 5. 1940s

We Love The 90's

The high street in the 90s looked very different to the highstreets of today – many of the biggest shops that you could find in almost any town now no longer exist! But how many shops do YOU remember?

Were you a Tammy Girl, spending hours shopping for graphic butterfly tops? Or maybe you loved shopping in Morgan, trying to find the perfect pair of jet-black kick flares? Or was Jane Norman's huge range of embellished jeans more your vibe?

If shopping for clothes wasn't so much your forte, perhaps you remember getting lost in the aisles at blockbuster, trying to pick out the perfect VHS for you and your friends to watch on a Friday night after school? Or for the artier of teens, maybe you loved going to Athena and flicking through the seemingly limitless collection of posters and wall art to cover your bedroom in?

Try your hand at these fun questions, to see how much of a shopaholic you were in the 90s!

1. There was a shoe shop beginning with 'R' where people went for slightly more posh footwear – what was it called?

2. What legendary high-street powerhouse used to have an equally legendary pick-n-mix aisle, before it sadly left our high-streets in 2008?

3. Which two letter shop were you always dragged to by your parents (for sensible clothes) that now can only be found in mainland Europe?

1. Ravel 2. Woolworths 3. C&A

Hailed as one of the most influential directors and writers of the 20th and 21st centuries, Tarantino's directorial debut in 1992 makes him one of the most important directors of the decade!

Within 8 years, by the end of the decade, his films had already been nominated for countless awards, and are still favourites amongst many!

As a director of blockbuster hits such as Pulp Fiction and Reservoir Dogs, and writer for Natural Born Killers and From Dusk Till Dawn, Tarantino is believed by many to be the most influential filmmaker of the 90s!

## Are you a Tarantino fan? Test your knowledge!

1. Which movie did Tarantino release in 1992?

2. Who was the actress who played The Bride in Kill Bill?

3. In From Dusk Till Dawn, what adult establishment features in the film?

1. Reservoir Dogs 2. Uma Thurman 3. Strip Club

90's PARTY

Quiz your friends and family!

In 1995, the biggest selling single of the year may give you a sense of déjà vu... think back to 1990. Sang by duo Robson & Jerome, on an episode of UK television drama Soldier Soldier in November 1994, performing as The Unrighteous Brothers, they sang a cover of Unchained Melody.

In 1995, this was released as a single, alongside White Cliffs of Dover, and this proved to be a hit in the charts, becoming the biggest selling single of the year! It's almost as if people in the 90s couldn't get enough of this 1965 classic!

## The rest of the charts looked like this:

1. UNCHAINED MELODY/WHITE CLIFFS OF DOVER - ROBSON & JEROME
2. GANGSTA'S PARADISE - COOLIO FEATURING L.V.
3. I BELIEVE/UP ON THE ROOF - ROBSON & JEROME
4. BACK FOR GOOD - TAKE THAT
5. THINK TWICE - CELINE DION
6. EARTH SONG - MICHAEL JACKSON
7. FAIRGROUND - SIMPLY RED
8. MISSING - EVERYTHING BUT THE GIRL
9. YOU ARE NOT ALONE - MICHAEL JACKSON
10. WONDERWALL - OASIS

# NINETIES IN OUR HEARTS

**Test out your knowledge of the 1995 smash hits — how much do you really know?**

1. Gangsta's Paradise was famously covered by which spoof musician, in a song called Amish Paradise?

2. Coming in at number 17 on the charts, Cotton Eyed Joe was sung by which group?

3. Peaking at number 2 on the charts, and finishing overall in 27th place, Diana King's song stated "I don't want no fly guy, I just want a _____"

4. Formally a member of The Sugarcubes, who had a 1995 hit with It's Oh So Quiet?

5. How many members of Take That were there?

1. "Weird Al" Yankovic 2. Rednex 3. Shy Guy 4. Bjork 5. 5

90's FOREVER

Any 1990s dinner party would be lost without the humble arctic roll – a favourite amongst school dinners and home cooks alike, the arctic roll dominated British cuisine, and made a huge impact on desserts we eat today!

Ingredients:
3 x eggs (medium)
100g golden caster sugar
100g self-raising white flour
1tsp (teaspoon) vanilla extract
500ml ice cream
250g strawberry jam

## Method:

Preheat your oven to 200°C (220°C fan / Gas Mark 6) and line a thin baking tray with baking paper.

Put your ice cream into a bowl then beat it until it becomes softer and mouldable. Place the ice cream onto baking paper and roll it into a long sausage. Wrap it up and refreeze for at least 1 hour.

Whisk together the 3 eggs and golden caster sugar until the mixture is pale. After, gently sift in the flour and begin to 'fold' it into the mixture. Add 1 tablespoon of water and fold this in also.

Pour the mixture onto the baking tray, and bake for 10-12 minutes (or until golden brown and firm).

Place some baking paper onto the worktop and sprinkle it with caster sugar. Turn the sponge onto this paper, and peel off the baking paper which was on the bottom of the sponge. Let this cool a little.

Trim the two longer sides of the sponge a little into straight lines (to remove crispy edges). Spread jam over the sponge, leaving a small gap near the edges.

Now it's time for ice cream! Bring out the ice cream and position it across the sponge. Using the baking paper underneath, roll the sponge around the ice cream.

Serve instantly!

Name: John Major
Born: 29th March 1943
Occupations: Politician
Notable Roles: Prime Minister of the United Kingdom

Sir John Major was the most prominent politician of the 1990s for the UK, as he was leader of the Conservative Party and Prime Minister from 1990 through till 1997. After John Major, in 1997, the country decided to change their tact and went with controversial Labour Leader Tony Blair, who was Prime Minister from 1997 to 2007 – impressive!

## Test your knowledge of UK politics in the 90s here!

1. In 1990, when John Major was elected into office, who was the leader of Labour, the primary opposition party?

2. What unusual job did John Major's father do whilst he was growing up? HINT: a performer of some kind.

3. One of the major successes of John Major's government was their peace work done with which Irish organisation?

1. Neil Kinnock 2. Circus Performer 3. IRA (Irish Republican Army)

Portable music player technology drastically changed in the 1990s, and saw millions of people around the world able to suddenly listen to their own personal music on the go, without the need for radio and other bulkier players! Whilst portable music players were also popular in other decades previously, things became smaller and more affordable in the 1990s!

In the early 1990s, the iconic Sony Walkman's popularity was still sky-high, after its booming success in the 1980s. However, a newer form of music player was taking advantage of more modern technology – the Sony Discman was now a portable CD player, which was seen as a more modern version of the Walkman itself. Although introduced in the 80s, this was more affordable and popular than ever before in the 1990s!

In the late 1990s, portable music technology forever changed on the introduction of the portable MP3 player, which allowed songs to be uploaded onto a small device, without the need to carry around CDs or cassettes!

What did you use to listen to music in the 1990s?

90s architecture was focused on breaking records with buildings becoming bigger and better than ever! There was also a particular focus on futuristic shapes and unique building designs, as creativity became popular over the cold, concrete brutalist styles that were the craze in the 70s and 80s! The 90s saw the erection of many iconic buildings around the world!

Here are some of the shining stars and record breakers:

### Petronas Towers – Kuala Lumpur
The Petronas Twin Towers began construction on the 1st March 1993, opening to the public on the 31st August 1999. Costing approximately $1.6 billion, these towers were designed by architect César Pelli, and until 2004, held the title of the tallest building in the world!

### O2 Arena – London
Now known as the O2 Arena, this structure was originally completed in 1999, and called 'The Millennium Dome'. Opening to the public on New Year's Eve, this was designed as a turning point for architecture in London, signalling a new step into futuristic designs!

### Guggenheim Museum – Bilbao
Designed by American architect Frank Gehry, the Guggenheim museum is a museum of modern and contemporary art, that was opened in 1997. One of the first of its kind, this curvy building was seen as one of the most spectacular modern buildings in the world, and seems to fold into the local landscape!

**90's TRIVIA**

## Test your knowledge on the below 90's architecture with this quiz!

1. The Guggenheim museum is one of how many other Guggenheim museums in the world?

2. In what country can the Petronas Towers be found?

3. What's the name of the area of London in which the O2 Arena can be found?

4. What is the tallest building in the world currently?

5. Another building famous for its architecture in the 90s was the Getty Museum - in which major US city can this building be found?

1. 5 2. Malaysia 3. Greenwich 4. Burj Khalifa, Dubai 5. Los Angeles

As always, the popular fashions of the 90s are a defining feature of the decade, with many memories being rooted in the clothes people wore! Having recently made a comeback in mainstream fashion, let's take a trip down memory lane and remember some of the popular clothing trends from the 90s, some of which are still popular today!

A unisex trend that was hugely popular in the 90s was baggy clothes — everything from oversized t shirts and shirts to wide-legged jeans, the slouchier the better! Made popular by the hip-hop and skater culture in the 90s, people soon found themselves sizing up a few sizes to stay on trend!

Fresh from the hyper-popular 80s shell suits, branded sportswear became the craze in the 90s! Swapping neon for more toned-down looks, everyone from locals in the pub to A-List celebrities, began donning branded tracksuits and casual trainers — perhaps influencing the athleisure trends of the 21st century!

Another staple of any 90s wardrobe was tie-dye! Whether it was a rainbow spiral, bleached swirl or meticulous pattern, the 90s saw this colourful trend make a comeback! Originating in the 1960s and heavily associated with the hippie movement, tie dye was seen as 'vintage' in the 90s, much as how 90s staples such as dungarees, strappy tops an baggy jumpers are popular today!

# 90's TRIVIA

**Think you were a fashionista in the 90s? See how much you really know!**

1. Influenced by the 1995 film Clueless, what colour plaid was made popular in the 90s?

2. Which Irish girl group was famed for their double denim image?

3. Iconic wide-legged jeans brand JNCO stood for 'Judge None, ____ ____'?

4. Shania Twain was famed for wearing which animal print?

5. Which celebrity couple famously wore matching double denim outfits in 2001?

1. Yellow 2. B*witched 3. Choose One 4. Leopard print 5. Britney Spears and Justin Timberlake

**90's PARTY**

Quiz your friends and family!

1996 saw many legendary songs reach pole position on the UK charts, including Oasis' Don't Look Back In Anger, Mark Morrison's Return Of The Mack, and possibly most shockingly, narrowly missing out on the top spot of biggest selling single with 1.16m sales, the Spice Girl's iconic debut, Wannabe. Coming in first position, with 1.17m in sales, was The Fugee's Killing Me Softly - what a year for music!

## Check out the top 10 songs of 1996 below!

1. KILLING ME SOFTLY - FUGEES
2. WANNABE - SPICE GIRLS
3. SPACEMAN - BABYLON ZOO
4. SAY YOU'LL BE THERE - SPICE GIRLS
5. 2 BECOME 1 - SPICE GIRLS
6. RETURN OF THE MACK - MARK MORRISON
7. THREE LIONS - BADDIEL/SKINNER/LIGHTNING SEED
8. OOH AAH... JUST A LITTLE BIT - GINA G
9. CHILDREN - ROBERT MILES
10. MYSTERIOUS GIRL - PETER ANDRE FT BUBBLER RANX

# NINETIES IN OUR HEARTS

**Was 1996 YOUR year in music? Take the quiz to find out:**

1. Who was the lead singer of the Fugees?

2. The Spice Girls famously all had nicknames, what were they?

3. In the song Three Lions, what's the legendary football chant they use in the opening line?

4. Coming in at number 24 of the year's top 40, Born Slippy by Underworld was famously featured on which Ewan McGregor film?

5. In the lyrics of Oasis' Don't Look Back In Anger, what's the name of the girl that 'can wait' and 'knows it's too late'?

1. Lauryn Hill 2. Scary Spice, Sporty Spice, Ginger Spice, Baby Spice, Posh Spice 3. It's Coming Home 4. Trainspotting 5. Sally

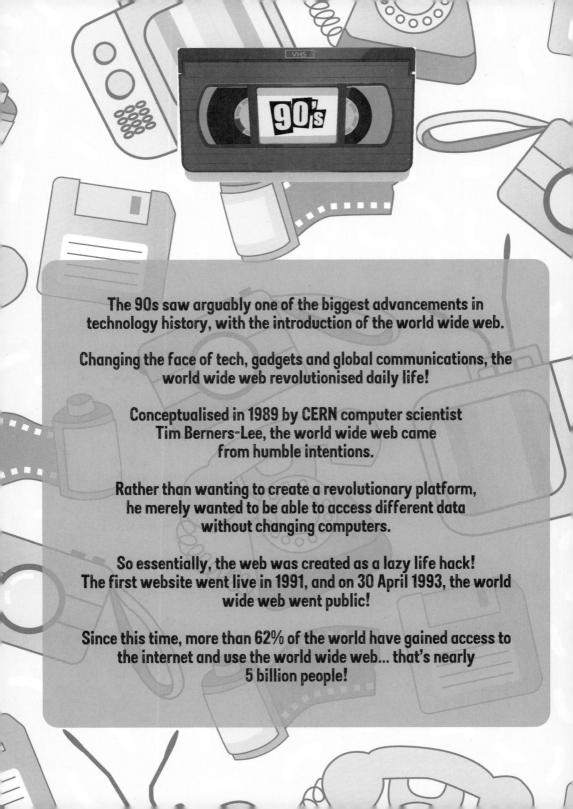

The 90s saw arguably one of the biggest advancements in technology history, with the introduction of the world wide web.

Changing the face of tech, gadgets and global communications, the world wide web revolutionised daily life!

Conceptualised in 1989 by CERN computer scientist Tim Berners-Lee, the world wide web came from humble intentions.

Rather than wanting to create a revolutionary platform, he merely wanted to be able to access different data without changing computers.

So essentially, the web was created as a lazy life hack! The first website went live in 1991, and on 30 April 1993, the world wide web went public!

Since this time, more than 62% of the world have gained access to the internet and use the world wide web... that's nearly 5 billion people!

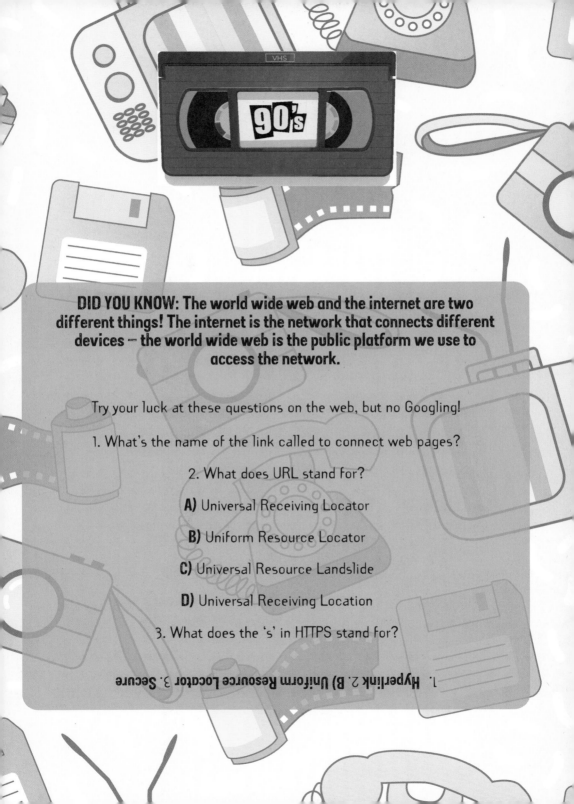

**DID YOU KNOW:** The world wide web and the internet are two different things! The internet is the network that connects different devices – the world wide web is the public platform we use to access the network.

Try your luck at these questions on the web, but no Googling!

1. What's the name of the link called to connect web pages?

2. What does URL stand for?

**A)** Universal Receiving Locator

**B)** Uniform Resource Locator

**C)** Universal Resource Landslide

**D)** Universal Receiving Location

3. What does the 's' in HTTPS stand for?

1. Hyperlink 2. B) Uniform Resource Locator 3. Secure

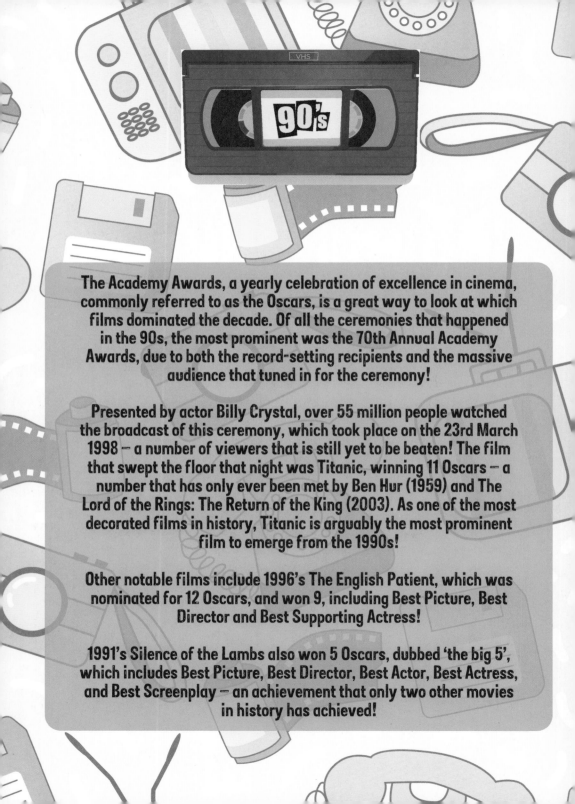

The Academy Awards, a yearly celebration of excellence in cinema, commonly referred to as the Oscars, is a great way to look at which films dominated the decade. Of all the ceremonies that happened in the 90s, the most prominent was the 70th Annual Academy Awards, due to both the record-setting recipients and the massive audience that tuned in for the ceremony!

Presented by actor Billy Crystal, over 55 million people watched the broadcast of this ceremony, which took place on the 23rd March 1998 – a number of viewers that is still yet to be beaten! The film that swept the floor that night was Titanic, winning 11 Oscars – a number that has only ever been met by Ben Hur (1959) and The Lord of the Rings: The Return of the King (2003). As one of the most decorated films in history, Titanic is arguably the most prominent film to emerge from the 1990s!

Other notable films include 1996's The English Patient, which was nominated for 12 Oscars, and won 9, including Best Picture, Best Director and Best Supporting Actress!

1991's Silence of the Lambs also won 5 Oscars, dubbed 'the big 5', which includes Best Picture, Best Director, Best Actor, Best Actress, and Best Screenplay – an achievement that only two other movies in history has achieved!

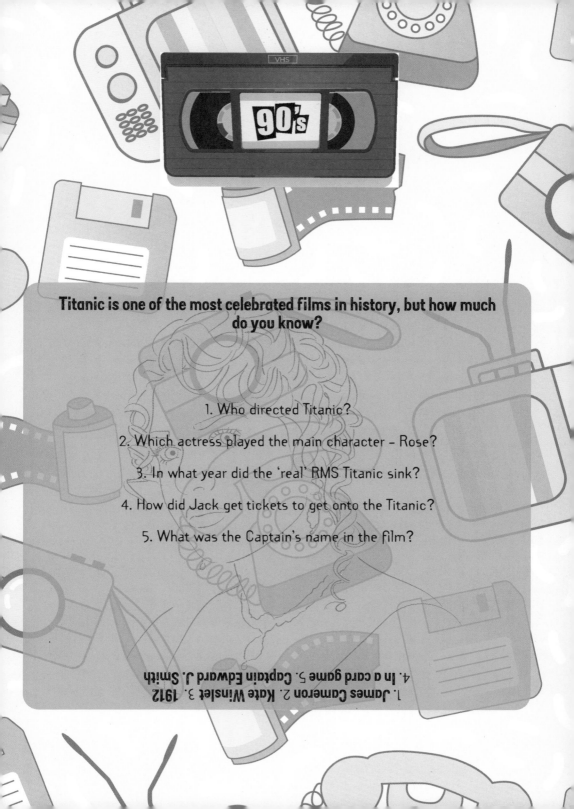

**VHS**

**90's**

## Titanic is one of the most celebrated films in history, but how much do you know?

1. Who directed Titanic?

2. Which actress played the main character – Rose?

3. In what year did the 'real' RMS Titanic sink?

4. How did Jack get tickets to get onto the Titanic?

5. What was the Captain's name in the film?

1. James Cameron 2. Kate Winslet 3. 1912 4. In a card game 5. Captain Edward J. Smith

In 1994, the opening of the Channel Tunnel was huge news, as this became the only fixed link between Great Britain and mainland Europe – and to this day this is still the case! Also called the Eurotunnel, this 50km long track runs beneath the English Channel, and the tunnel is the longest undersea rail portion of any tunnel in the world! Digging began in 1987 and was completed in 1991, before official building began.

The Channel Tunnel helped massively increase the movement of international travel between the UK and mainland Europe, and cost a whopping £4.65 billion, which was 80 percent more than was originally expected! Now classed as one of the seven wonders of the modern world, it's safe to see that the investment has certainly paid off!

**Have you ever used the Channel Tunnel?**

**See how much you know about this underwater landmark with these fascinating questions:**

1. Which two towns/cities are connected via the Channel Tunnel?

2. To the nearest 100m, how long is the train?

3. What kind of rock is the tunnel drilled into?

1. Folkestone and Calais 2. 400m 3. Chalk

# 90's TRIVIA

Test your decade knowledge with these fun 90s trivia questions. Remember, all of these are pot luck, so could be about any year and any topic — let's see how much of a 90s kid you really are!

1. Recently rebooted on Channel 4, what was the name of the TV show that two teams compete at DIY?

2. Who was the Prime Minister at the start of the 90s in the UK?

3. Who beat England out of the 1998 Fifa World Cup finals in France on penalties?

4. Pulp released their single Common People in 1995. But which city in the UK are the band from?

5. In which 90s movie did Harrison Ford play the role of President James Marshall –
**A)** American Beauty, **B)** Indiana Jones and the Last Crusade, **C)** Saving Private Ryan, **D)** Air Force One

1. Changing Rooms 2. John Major 3. Argentina 4. Sheffield 5. D) Air Force One

Name: Mariah Carey
Born: 27th March 1969
Occupations: Singer, Songwriter, Actress
Biggest-Selling Hit: All I Want For Christmas Is You

**Born in Huntington, New York, Mariah Carey shot to fame in 1990, after her first ever live performance, singing 'America the Beautiful' at the NBA finals. Her debut self-titled album topped the Billboard 200 for 11 consecutive weeks, after her success at the Grammys. From this moment, she went on to be one of the biggest selling female vocalists of all time, beaten only by Rihanna, Celine Dion and Madonna. Billboard named her the voice of the 1990s, and it's clear to see why!**

## How much do you know about this legendary pop diva?

1. In 1998, Mariah Carey recorded 'When You Believe' for the film The Prince of Egypt with which other singer?

2. What does Mariah Carey call her fans, which particularly rose to light in the 2000s?

3. How many octaves is Mariah Carey's vocal range?

4. The piercingly high notes that Mariah Carey sang are called what?

5. Which rapper does Mariah Carey famously have a feud with, that inspired her song 'Obsessed'?

**1. Whitney Houston 2. Lambs 3. 5 Octaves 4. Whistle notes 5. Eminem**

When looking at CGI advancements in the 1990s, we need to look no further than everyone's loved animated film –1995s Toy Story. An instant classic, this film introduced us to animated characters that are still firm favourites, such as Woody the cowboy and Buzz Lightyear, the hero astronaut.

However, did you know that this film was the first full-length feature film to be completely CGI animated? This is why most of the characters are wearing hats or have short hair – it's because hair is extremely difficult to animate, so the less of it – the better! At the time of its release, it became the third highest grossing animated film ever, behind Aladdin and the Lion King!

**Test your Toy Story knowledge here!**

1. True or false: Toy Story was Pixar's first full feature length film.

2. Who voices Woody?

3. How many Toy Story movies are there in total?

4. What is the name of the raspy penguin in the franchise?

5. What's the name of the child who owns Woody, Buzz and the majority of the other main toys?

1. True 2. Tom Hanks 3. 4 4. Wheezy 5. Andy

In 1997, after the tragic death of Princess Diana, Elton John re-recorded another version of his 1974 single Candle In The Wind, intended to be played at Diana's funeral. Released as a single the following week, Something About The Way You Look/Candle In the Wind sold 4.77 million copies by the end of 1997, and spent a total of 5 weeks at number one!

To this day, this song remains the biggest selling single since UK and US charts began in the 50s, amassing over 33 million sales!

## The UK top 10 of 1997 looked like this:

1. SOMETHING ABOUT THE WAY YOU LOOK/CANDLE IN THE WIND - ELTON JOHN
2. BARBIE GIRL - AQUA
3. I'LL BE MISSING YOU - PUFF DADDY & FAITH EVANS
4. PERFECT DAY - VARIOUS ARTISTS
5. TELETUBBIES SAY EH-OH! - TELETUBBIES
6. MEN IN BLACK - WILL SMITH
7. DON'T SPEAK - NO DOUBT
8. TORN - NATALIE IMBRUGLIA
9. SPICE UP YOUR LIFE - SPICE GIRLS
10. TUBTHUMPING – CHUMBAWAMBA

# NINETIES IN OUR HEARTS

**As we near the noughties, how much do you know about the hits from 1997?**

1. In the chorus of Aqua's Barbie Girl, what 2 actions does Barbie give permission to do?

2. What were the names of the 4 Teletubbies?

3. Who is the lead singer of No Doubt?

4. Perfect Day was a cover of a 1972 song, released as a charity single for Comic Relief. Who sang the original?

5. In Tubthumping, can you name one of the drinks that feature in the song's lyrics?

1. Brush her hair, undress her everywhere. 2. Tinky Winky, Dipsy, La La, Po
3. Gwen Stefani 4. Lou Reed 5. Whiskey, Vodka, Lager, Cider

90s fashion would be incomplete without its accessories — from signature hats, bags and glasses to hair accessories and jewellery, the 1990s was a decade filled with iconic outfit add-ons that every kid wanted!

Here are a few fashion accessories that blew up in the 90s, and can still be seen today!

### The Bucket Hat

One of the most signature accessories of the 90s was the bucket hat. Although its history extends back to the early 1900s, the bucket hat was brought into street style in the late 80s, and stuck around through the 90s, as it was seen on many rappers and Brit-pop icons throughout the decade! Resurfacing as part of festival fashion in recent years, it's clear to see that some fashion trends will never die down!

### The Choker

A type of necklace that sat tight around the neck, the choker was actually popular in the 1920s, but resurfaced as part of the grunge movement in the early 90s. The infamous tattoo choker was the must-have accessory for every it-girl, and from there, styles branched out into every group of society - even Princess Diana can be seen wearing a pearl variety!

### Hoop Earrings

Hoop earrings have been around for thousands of years - in ancient Egypt both men and women wore heavily embellished gold hoops to symbolise power and wealth. Whilst being popular in the 60s and 70s also, they emerged into the mainstream in the 90s, becoming a staple accessory of the decade! With hip-hop and Latina culture having a greater mainstream influence than ever before!

## 90's TRIVIA

**Test your knowledge of the must-have accessories of the 1990s – were you as cool as you think you were?**

1. Not worn on the back, what kind of bags were popular in the 1990s rave scene?

2. Iconic colourful oval-shaped glasses were made popular in the 1990s because of which male singer?

3. What hair tie was popular in the 90s? P.S – they came in all patterns, materials and colours!

4. What ancient Chinese black and white symbol was a popular feature of 90s jewellery?

5. What animal were the small, multicoloured hair-clips shaped like, that were popular in the 1990s?

1. **Bum Bags / Fanny Packs** 2. **Kurt Cobain** 3. **A: Scrunchies**
4. **Yin Yang symbol** 5. **Butterfly**

If you grew up in the 1990s, then the likelihood is you had a packed lunch. Not only that, but there was almost that one person in your class who always had the cool lunch snacks, that you just weren't allowed to have – no matter how hard you begged!

If you were really lucky, maybe on a birthday or special occasion, you were allowed Lunchables. That small, plastic tray filled with plastic cheese and plastic ham and sweet, cardboard crackers sounds kinda gross, and yet was the most delicious thing you could wish for when you opened your lunchbox.

As a snack, perhaps you wanted a Cheesestring? Entering the snack world in 1996, Cheesestrings dominated lunchboxes of the 90s, partially because they were seen as a healthier snack to some of the greasier, saltier options, and so was something you could ask for that you may actually be able to get!

As a sweet snack, perhaps a tube of yoghurt in the form of a Frube? Or maybe a packet of Cadbury's animal biscuits were your kryptonite?

If you had it your way, to drink, would you have chosen a Capri Sun? That good small squeezy pouch of fruit juice really tested like liquid nectar. Or maybe you were more of an Um Bongo kid, because of the fun animal-themed design of the cartons?

What did your dream lunchbox look like?

# NINETIES IN OUR HEARTS

**How much do you remember about 90s lunch boxes? Maybe you preferred school dinners?**

1. Everyone's favourite ham was in the shape of a bear, but what was its name?

2. The popular snack, Wagon Wheels, were a prominent feature of kids lunchboxes in the 1990s, but in which decade were they invented?

3. What animal was everyone's favourite biscuit bar named after?

4. Name 3 flavours of Space Raider crisps (4 available).

5. What was the name of the popular crisp that you could turn into a car-like shape?

1. Billy Bear 2. 1940s 3. Penguin 4. Pickled Onion, Beef, Spicy, Saucy BBQ 5. Transform-A-Snack

**The 1990s saw many world records beaten – ranging from impressive sporting accolades to awesome stunts, let's take a look back at some of the most impressive stunts and records that were smashed in the 1990s!**

1. In 1992, 19 year old Bryan Berg built a record-breaking 75 storey house of cards, breaking the world record for the tallest house of cards! This is a record that he would then go on to break a further 9 times!

2. In 1993, a Scotsman named Campell Aird became the first man in history with a bionic arm!

3. In 1995, the Boomerang Nebula was discovered to be the coldest location in the Milky Way galaxy – and is still unbeaten! Located 5000 light years away, temperatures here measured a staggering -272 degrees Celsius... brrrrrr!

4. In 1999, Jay Ohrberg from California broke the record for the world's longest car, with a 26 wheeled limo, that featured a swimming pool and a king size bed!

90's TRIVIA

Try your luck at these fun questions on the crazy, record-breaking events of the decade!

1. In 1997, the record was broken for the fastest car measured over one mile in Nevada. To the nearest 100mph, how fast was the car going?

2. In 1998, the record was broken for the longest escalator ride, but to the nearest 20 miles, how far was the distance Suresh Joachim travelled on escalators at a shopping centre in Australia?

3. In 1994, Daniel Bent broke the record for the fastest time to complete the world _____ snorkelling championships – in what unconventional terrain was he snorkelling in?

4. To the nearest 10ft, how long was Jay Ohrberg's record-breaking stretched limo?

1. 800mph (762.035mph) 2. 140 miles! 3. Bog 4. 100 ft

Cars that were popular in the 1990s are largely unrecognisable from their modern-day counterparts, with boxier shapes and more neutral colours being the favourites amongst British drivers, and drivers worldwide.

The bestselling car of the 90s actually remains in the top 10 cars today — the humble Ford Fiesta! With well over a million sold during the decade — the Ford Fiesta now looks very different to the 90s model, but you may still spot some of the old ones, with nearly 200,000 remaining!

Another car introduced in the 1990s was the Renault Clio — emerging in 1990, the Clio became an instant success, and has remained at the top of the popularity boards ever since!

Voted European Car of the Year, once in 1991 and again in 2006, roads of the 1990s would be incomplete without the humble Renault Clio!

If you had a little more to spend, and wanted to be a little flashier, then in 1993, Mercedes introduced the C-Class.

A sleek and sophisticated car, this was a favourite of the middle classes, and would set you back around £30,000! Sadly, the first generation of this car ceased production in 2000, making it exclusively a car of the 1990s!

# 90's TRIVIA

**See if you're a true petrol head with these fun questions on the most popular cars of the decade:**

1. Coming from the Latin word for 'star', what model of Vauxhall was popular in the 90s?

2. Driven by Pierce Brosnan in 'Goldeneye', which BMW car was hugely popular in the 1990s?

3. What popular Volkswagen car shares its name with a popular sport?

4. What iconic green car did Mr Bean drive?

5. Plural for 'micron' the Micra was a popular model of which car manufacturer?

1. Astra 2. 3 series (E36) 3. Golf 4. Mini (exact model – applejack green 1976 Mini 1000 MkII) 5. Nissan

**Quiz your friends and family!**

After what had been a rather depressing set of 'best-selling singles' for the past 8 years, 1998 finally picked up the pace, with Cher's comeback hit Believe. Using new autotune technology, Cher was able to break records and redefine her sound nearly 30 years into her career, making Believe the first song by a female solo artist to be certified Triple Platinum, selling over 1.5m copies!

The real question is...do YOU believe in life after love?

## The overall top 10 singles of 1998 were as follows:

1. BELIEVE - CHER
2. MY HEART WILL GO ON - CELINE DION
3. IT'S LIKE THAT - RUN DMC VS. JASON NEVINS
4. NO MATTER WHAT - BOYZONE
5. C'EST LA VIE - B*WITCHED
6. HOW DO I LIVE - LEANN RIMES
7. CHOCOLATE SALTY BALLS (PS I LOVE YOU) - CHEF
8. GOODBYE - SPICE GIRLS
9. GHETTO SUPASTAR (THAT IS WHAT YOU ARE) - PRAS MICHEL FT. ODB AND MYA
10. TRULY MADLY DEEPLY - SAVAGE GARDEN

# NINETIES IN OUR HEARTS

**Test yourself on your 1997 music knowledge with these 5 fun questions!**

1. Just missing out at a spot in the top 10 was the club hit by Starlight. Finish the title: Music Sounds Better _____?

2. Steps came in at 12th spot on the year end charts with Heartbeat/Tragedy. How many members were there in the group?

3. The Boy is Mine is an R&B duet between which two female artists?

4. What decade was Cher born?

5. Chocolate Salty Balls (PS I Love You) was a song from which TV series?

1. With You 2. 5 3. Brandy & Monica 4. 1940s 5. South Park

**We Love The 90's**

The 90s saw many hairstyle trends popular amongst women, but what were some of the major styles that everyone seemed to want, inspired by celebrities, musicians, and TV and film, but how many of these do you remember?

One of the major 90s hair trends that was popular was the pixie cut. Seen as short and sleek, celebrities like Winona Ryder showed how fashionable and versatile this hairstyle could be! This was made more popular through the grunge and androgynous trends that were big in the 90s for women, with a more tomboyish style being all the rage!

Another hugely popular style was called the 'Rachel', and is characterised by choppy, voluminous layers and subtle honey highlights. This hairstyle is still popular today, showing that not all trends have an expiration date!

The bob was also super-fashionable in the 1990s, with pop-group megastar Victoria Beckham inspiring girls around the world to get this shoulder-skimming cut!

How well do you know 90s hair — with many inspirations from TV and film, can you connect the dots?

1. The pixie cut was famously rocked by which actress, in the 90s film 'Ghost'?

2. Given its name, the 'Rachel' was inspired by which TV show?

3. Cameron Diaz rocked a bob in which 90s rom-com?

1. Demi Moore 2. Friends 3. There's Something About Mary

# 90's TRIVIA

The 90s is arguably the decade where the term 'Supermodel' became widely used! Ordinary fashion models became celebrities in their own rights, and started to demand higher pay to feature in magazine spreads and runway shows. Many of the trend-setting household model names we know and love today shot to fame in the 1990s, such as Naomi Campbell, Kate Moss and Linda Evangelista, to name a few!

## How much do you know about the world of supermodels in the 1990s?

1. Starting on the 1st August 1995, which brand's annual lingerie fashion show became iconic for featuring supermodels in its runway and advertising campaign?

2. Which famous 90s model went on to create the TV series 'America's Next Top Model'?

3. What is the nationality of Linda Evangelista?

4. Which 90s supermodel made headlines in 2007 when she famously threw a phone at her assistant?

5. Which brand's black and white 90s fashion campaign featured celebrities and models such as Mark Whalberg and Kate Moss, donning underwear and denim?

1. Victoria's Secret 2. Tyra Banks 3. Canadian
4. Naomi Campbell 5. Calvin Klein

The 1990s can be hailed the decade of the sitcom, with plenty of iconic series launching, many of which are still watched around the world today! These include Sex and the City, The Fresh Prince of Bel Air and Boy Meets World. One of the most successful, however, is Friends, which is still adored by many!

Set in New York City, Friends was so successful because it showed the lives of young, somewhat single, mixed gender adults, and was not centred on romance or family values and structures. This revolutionised the sitcom aspect, appealing to a much wider audience due to its relatability, humour and gender neutral aspects!

Friends, launched the careers of now Hollywood A-Listers such as Jennifer Anniston, Matt LeBlanc and Courtney Cox! Launching in 1994, Friends aired 236 episodes over a 10 year period - bad news for Friends haters!

Were you a Friends fan, or was the series your foe?

**Test your Friends knowledge to find out if you were a true fan!**

1. What was the iconic Friends theme song?

2. How many main characters were there in friends?

3. Which Fashion Brand did Rachel get a job with in Paris?

4. What was Monica's surname?

5. How many sisters did Joey have?
A) 2
B) 4
C) 7
C) None

1. I'll Be There For You – The Rembrandts 2. 6 3. Louis Vuitton 4. Geller 5. C) 7

**90's TRIVIA**

The way people chose to decorate their homes in the 1990s is great at sparking some memories of 90s culture!

Much like the clothes people wore, the 1990s experienced a great shift in interior design trends that reflected attitudes towards fashion, lifestyle changes and pop-culture trends! How many do you remember though?

## 1. Inflatable furniture

After their introduction in the 1960s, inflatable furniture sales seemed to deflate in the 70s and 80s - much like the furniture itself!

However, in the 90s, its popularity blew up again! With everything from inflatable armchairs and tables to loungers and whole beds, inflatable furniture was popular amongst teenagers around the world!

## 2. Animal Print

Inspired by the runways of Roberto Cavalli and Versace, two hugely popular designers of the 1990s, animal print spread like wildfire, and no home was safe.

From cushions and other soft furnishings, to curtains and wallpaper, every animal print imaginable could be seen in homes up and down the country!

### 3. Minimalism

To challenge the garish prints that were becoming popular, minimalism also saw a rise in popularity in the 90s! Inspired by elements of Chinese and Japanese styles, people forewent the maximalism of the 80s for more neutral colours and tones!

### 4. Fake Plants

Peaking in popularity in the 1990s, plastic plants were EVERYWHERE. From shiny green ivy to fabric orchids, homes became covered with plants that could add a pop of colour without the prospect of them dying – a horticulturists worst nightmare! This trend, although dying down, is still popular today – just take a trip to IKEA!

### Trivia:

1. Released in 1995, who released a song called 'Fake Plastic Trees'?

2. What was the four-letter word for the lighting that was usually bright-coloured, formed of gas-filled electrified tubes, popular in the 1990s?

3. What was used to achieve a mottled, free-form effect on walls that was popular in the 90s?

1. Radiohead 2. Neon 3. Sponge

**The 1990s saw many ground-breaking scientific discoveries and achievements, many of which we now take for granted and couldn't live without! Here are 5 examples of scientific events that made headlines throughout the decade!**

1. On the 14th January 1992, the first baby conceived through IVF (short for 'in vitro fertilisation') was born! The baby was conceived by injecting a single sperm cell into an unfertilised egg, and is now common practice for people all over the world!

2. In 1995, the Global Positioning System (GPS) became fully operational and available worldwide, which has since allowed for daily features such as Google Maps and Satnavs to be common place around the world – no more getting lost!

3. In 1996, the infamous Dolly the sheep made headlines worldwide, as she was the first adult mammal successfully cloned from an adult cell. She was cloned by Keith Campbell and Ian Wilmut, of the University of Edinburgh!

**TRIVIA**

How much do you know about the scientific discoveries of the decade? Test your knowledge with these fun questions:

1. How many years did Dolly the Sheep live, before she was euthanized due to a progressive lung disease?

2. In 1996, which out-of-space structure began construction?

3. In December 1995, the Galileo probe orbited which planet, allowing for greater studies into its surface and moons?

4. Which large telescope was launched in the 90s that revolutionised astronomy?

5. Which healthy food, called the Flavr Savr, was the first genetically modified version of its kind to get approved for sale to the public in the 1990s?

1. 6 years old 2. International Space Station 3. Jupiter 4. The Hubble Telescope 5. Tomato

Continuing on from Cher's dance-hit success, the biggest selling single of 1999 laid the groundwork for many high-tempo hits of the noughties! Britney Spears' now legendary debut hit ... Baby One More Time scored nearly 464k sales in its first week, making it the best-selling song of the year, foreshadowing her step into becoming a pop legend in the early 2000s!

## 1999 was a year filled with other iconic songs! Take a look at the year's top 10:

1. BABY ONE MORE TIME - BRITNEY SPEARS
2. BLUE (DA BA DEE) - EIFFEL 65
3. THE MILLENNIUM PRAYER - CLIFF RICHARD
4. MAMBO NO.5 (A LITTLE BIT OF...) - LOU BEGA
5. 9PM (TILL I COME) - ATB
6. LIVIN' LA VIDA LOCA - RICKY MARTIN
7. THAT DON'T IMPRESS ME MUCH - SHANIA TWAIN
8. SWEET LIKE CHOCOLATE - SHANKS & BIGFOOT
9. FLAT BEAT - MR. OIZO
10. WHEN THE GOING GETS TOUGH - BOYZONE

# NINETIES IN OUR HEARTS

**Test your knowledge of the 1999 charts with these 5 fun questions!**

1. Coming in at number 13 on the charts, Christina Aguilera sang which song? Think... Aladdin.

2. In Mambo No. 5, Lou Bega lists different female names. Fill the blank: 'A little bit of _____ in the sun'

3. If Britney's Baby One More Time was released towards the end of 1998, how old was Britney when she released it?

4. Eiffel 65 were formed in which country?

5. According to Ronan Keating, how do you say it best?

1. Genie in a Bottle 2. Sandra 3. Sixteen 4. Italy 5. When you say nothing at all

**90's FOREVER**

Whether you preferred banana, strawberry, chocolate or butterscotch, any 90s kid will remember their fixation on Angel Delight.

This simple, mousse-like dessert was quick, sweet and delicious, and experienced a massive boom in popularity in the 1990s due to an advertising push from the likes of none-other than Wallace and Gromit themselves.

Try this fun angel delight cheesecake to bring some sophistication to this childhood-favourite!

Ingredients:

For the cheesecake base:
150g biscuits (Digestives recommended, but you can use most biscuits of choice!)
80g unsalted butter, melted

For the cheesecake:
450g cream cheese
100g icing sugar
200ml double cream
2 sachets Angel Delight
(Choose your favourite!)

# NINETIES IN OUR HEARTS

## Method:

1. Line the sides and base of a cake tin with baking parchment – a tin of around 8 inches diameter is best!

2. Bash the biscuits until they're crumbs, and add in the melted butter, before pressing the mixture firmly into the base of the tin. Chill for 30 minutes.

3. Combine the cream cheese, sieved icing sugar, angel delight and double cream until smooth.

4. Tip into the cake tin, and chill until set.

5. Decorate it with your favourite toppings and enjoy (sprinkles recommended for the proper experience!)

**Test your decade knowledge with these fun 90s trivia questions. Remember, all of these are pot luck, so could be about any year and any topic – let's see how much of a 90s kid you really are!**

1. Which fashion designer was famously shot dead on the steps of his Miami beach mansion in 1997?

2. Which comedy film, released in 1993, featured a Jamaican bobsled team?

3. Which rapper did Madonna date briefly in 1992?

4. Where was Mount Pinatubo, a volcano that erupted, causing devastation?

1. Gianni Versace 2. Cool Runnings 3. Vanilla Ice 4. Philippines

**90's TRIVIA**

Test your knowledge of this iconic decade with these
fun true or false questions!

1. Tetris was the first video game to be played in space in the 90s.

2. The X-box was the best-selling video game console of the decade.

3. The world wide web was introduced in 1993.

4. The popular toy 'Furby' was accused of spying on people.

5. Beanie Babies were introduced in 1993.

1. True 2. False – The Sony PlayStation 3. False - 1991
4. True 5. True

## 90's TRIVIA

**Test your knowledge of this iconic decade with these fun true or false questions!**

6. Mike Tyson famously bit off an ear in 1997.

7. The Motorola was the most popular mobile phone in the 90s.

8. Spider clips were the most popular hair clip for girls in the 90s.

9. The Backstreet Boys had 6 members.

10. The group 'Aqua' got sued by Mattel for singing a song about Barbie.

6. True 7. False - The Nokia 3210 8. False – Butterfly clips 9. False - Five 10. True

**90's FOREVER**

Much like any decade in history, the 1990s is home to some lesser-known but wild, crazy and hilariously out-there facts and statistics that will really open your eyes!

1. Michael Jackson was such a huge fan of Spider-Man, and his lifelong dream was to be able to play him in a movie! So, in the 1990s, MJ tried to buy Marvel Comics, so he could make his dream a reality! He didn't succeed – of course.

2. In the 1990s, a national American survey found that more children could recognise Super Mario than Mickey Mouse, proving that video games were really starting to take over!

3. IMDb is actually one of the oldest websites on the internet, launching in 1990 as a website that listed actresses 'with beautiful eyes' – weird!

4. Two American airlines, Southwest Airlines and Stevens Aviation, both wanted to use the same slogan, but instead of settling it through court, the two CEOs arm wrestled to see which company would own the rights to it – Stevens Aviation won, but let Southwest keep the slogan... after all that!

5. The roar heard in Jurassic Park is actually the sound of a Jack Russel playing with a rope! The film crew slowed down this recording, and realised it sounded like a dinosaur, and used it in the film franchise!

## Can you guess the answers to these 90s statistics?

1. What was the population of the UK in 1990?

A) 49 million, B) 57 million, C) 61 million, D) 67 million

2. Approximately how many babies were born in the US in 1995?

A) 1,500,000, B) 2,600,000, C) 3,900,000, D) 4,700,000

3. What was the average price of petrol in the UK in 1992?

A) 27.4p, B) 40.3p, C) 58.4p, D) 77.2p

4. In 1998, what was the average life expectancy in the UK?

A) 62.3 years, B) 65.9 years, C) 74.1 years, D) 77.2 years

5. In 1993, what was the unemployment rate in the UK?

A) 10.4%, B) 8.1%, C) 5.9%, D) 4.2%

1. B) 57 Million 2. C) 3,900,000 3. B) 40.3p
4. D) 77.2 years 5. A) 10.4%

"Once you figure out who you are and what you love about yourself, I think it all kinda falls into place." – Jennifer Aniston

# 90's
## TRIVIA

There were many legendary movie quotes that came out in the 1990s, but how many of these do you know? See whether you know which film these quotes came from?

1. "Life is like a box of chocolates"

2. "Hope is a good thing, maybe the best of things. And no good thing ever dies."

3. "That'll do, pig."

4. "I know kung fu."

5. "Molly, you in danger, girl."

**How many did you get right? What's your favourite movie quote of the decade?**

1. Forrest Gump 2. Shawshank Redemption 3. Babe 4. The Matrix 5. Ghost

# NINETIES IN OUR HEARTS

# NINETIES IN OUR HEARTS

blur
versus
oasis

# NINETIES IN OUR HEARTS

# 90's TRIVIA

In 1998, British artist Tracey Emin first created her controversial modern sculpture, entitled 'My Bed'. A year later, in 1999, this was exhibited at the Tate Gallery, as one of the shortlisted pieces of art for the prestigious Turner Prize.

The sculpture consisted of an unmade, messy bed, which was surrounded by objects that you could find in Emin's bedroom, and was inspired by a depressive episode the artist had experienced.

Due to its seemingly simple creation, the artwork generated loads of media attention, with many people questioning whether the bed was actually art! However, when challenged with claims that anyone could exhibit an unmade bed, she responded simply with "Well they didn't, did they? No one had ever done that before."

**What's your opinion on this infamous piece of 90s artwork?**

**How much can you guess about this artist?**

1. What decade was Tracey Emin born?

2. In which southern English county did Emin grow up?

3. In 2014, how much was Emin's 'My Bed' sold for?

A) £3 million B) £1.2 million C) £2.5 million D) £4.6 million

1. 60s 2. Kent 3. C) £2.5 Million

Early on the 18th March 1990, one of the greatest art heists in history occurred at the Isabella Stewart Gardner Museum in Boston, Massachusetts! Unlike other notable museum thefts, this particular case remains unsolved to this day.

Two guards admitted that two men posed as police officers responding to a call-in about a disturbance, and were granted entry, before tying up the guards and proceeding to spend 1 hour robbing prized artworks from the museum.

Rare paintings by artists such as Vermeer, Rembrandt, Degas and Manet were taken in a haul that is now valued by the FBI at over $500 million! The museum itself is offering a $10 million for information that leads to the recovery of the stolen art — the largest reward ever offered by a private institution!

Suspects largely comprised of members of Boston's powerful gangs and conmen, but due to a lack of evidence, no one has been convicted. This remains one of the highest value heists in history, and has even inspired many documentaries and TV shows — notably Netflix's This Is a Robbery: The World's Biggest Art Heist.

Name: Damien Hirst
Born: 7th June 1965
Occupations: Artist, Entrepreneur
Most Notable Work: The Physical Impossibility of Death in the
Mind of Someone Living

Born Damien Steven Brennan, Hirst is one of the most famous and controversial artists of the 1990s, and actually holds the title for the richest living artist, with an estimated net worth of around $1 billion. Studying Fine Art at Goldsmiths University in London, Hirst shot to fame in 1991, when he created The Physical Impossibility of Death in the Mind of Someone Living, which was a Tiger Shark that was suspended in Formaldehyde – a format of work that would recur throughout his career!?

## How much do you know about Damien Hirst?
## Try your luck at these arty farty questions!

1. What prestigious art award did Hirst win in 1995?

2. Worth nearly £50 million, Damien Hirst's For the Love of God is a platinum cast of a human skull, covered with what?

3. What surprising grade did Hirst receive for his A-Level Art?

1. The Turner Prize 2. Diamonds 3. E

We Love The
90's

Bookworms in the 1990s were really in for a treat! Book releases in the 1990s have inspired everything, from on stage productions to billion-pound movie franchises... but which books were the most popular and iconic?

Published in 1996, Helen Fielding's Bridget Jones's Diary became an instant success and best seller. Centring on a hilariously loveable single woman trying to become a better version of herself, many people found this book to be refreshingly relatable!

Nicholas Sparks set hearts alight in 1996, with his passionate romance novel, The Notebook. Set in post-WWII North Carolina, this book has since become what is regarded as one of the best romance films of all time, and has caused enough tears to fill a lake... all thanks to Sparks!

J.K Rowling's Harry Potter and the Philosopher's Stone was first published in 1997, and was such a success, that it is hard to imagine our lives without it!

This book is responsible for an 8-part movie franchise, theme park and, most importantly, is credited as inspiring a new generation to fall in love with reading again!

**90's TRIVIA**

## How much do you know about some of the best-sellers of the 90s?

1. What is the name of the street that Harry Potter lived on?

2. In which city is Bridget Jones's Diary set?

3. Who played Noah in the 2004 cinematic rendition of Nicholas Sparks' The Notebook?

4. Written by Robert Ludlum, which book was published in 1990, and has since inspired an action film series, starring Matt Damon?

5. Tracy Chevalier wrote a 1999 novel, set in 17th century Holland, inspired by and named after, a Vermeer painting. What is the name of the novel: Girl With _____

1. **Privet Drive** 2. **London** 3. **Ryan Gosling** 4. **The Bourne Ultimatum** 5. **A Pearl Earring**

We Love The
# 90's

**Popular cars of the 90s!**

90's
FOREVER

"The lower you fall, the higher you'll fly."
– Chuck Palahniuk, 'Fight Club' (1999)

The French Martini has arguably become less popular in recent years, but during the 1990s, it became a trendy drink of choice for people around the world! Technically not a martini at all, it is comprised of three main ingredients: pineapple, vodka and black raspberry liqueur! Emerging in the late 1980s in New York.

Made popular in restauranteur Keith McNally's bars, the French Martini got its name because it was served in a martini glass, and used French liqueur Chambord. Spreading slowly in the early 90s, by 1996 it had reached bars all over the world, largely due to a massive advertising campaign by Chambord, the raspberry liqueur used in the martini!

**Have you ever tried a French Martini?**

# NINETIES IN OUR HEARTS

### Ingredients:

40ml Vodka

20ml Chambord Liqueur (or any raspberry liqueur of your choosing!)

60ml pineapple juice

### Method:

Shake all the ingredients in a cocktail shaker hard with ice, until the drink begins to froth, before straining into a glass. Garnish with a pineapple wedge and a few raspberries and enjoy!

Other variations are:

Le Frog (Swap the vodka with an equal amount of single malt whiskey)

Hot Tub (Add a splash of prosecco on top to bring the bubbles - hence the name!)

Myth, a sculpture by Damien Hirst.

There were many great comedies of the 1990s that were a staple of British TV, bringing many comedians that we know and love today into the limelight!

One of the Nation's favourites – Father Ted – first aired on the 21st April 1995 on Channel 4, and ran for three much-loved seasons, until its final episode on the 1st May 1998! Based around three chaotic priests who were banished to Craggy Island, a fictional location off the mainland of Ireland, and the wacky, wild and loveable situations that occurred there!

Another firm favourite of 90s telly was Absolutely Fabulous, which first aired on the 12th November 1992, and ran for an epic 5 seasons! Centred around two fashionable best friends, Patsy and Edina with addiction issues, Absolutely Fabulous helped to define British comedy as we know it today!

The 90s also saw us introduced to character Alan Partridge in the aptly named series, I'm Alan Partridge. Airing on the 3rd November 1997, this series followed a clueless radio host and his thirst for stardom, after getting dropped from the BBC. Running for one season in the 1990s, and resurfacing for another in 2002, Alan Partridge became a much-loved character amongst fans of British Comedy!

90's TRIVIA

## How much do you know about British Comedy?
## Test your knowledge here!

1. What hymn is sung during the opening credits of The Vicar of Dibley?

2. Which two actresses play the roles of Patsy and Edina in Absolutely Fabulous?

3. Where in the UK was The Royle Family set?

4. What was the name of the teenager played by Harry Enfield?

5. Running on BBC Two from 1994 to 1997, the sketch show that took a stab at various British stereotypes was called The _____ Show?

1. The Lord Is My Shephard 2. Joanna Lumley and Jennifer Saunders 3. Manchester 4. Kevin 5. Fast

**Mens 90's hairstyles.**

"Hakuna Matata. It means no worries."
— Pumbaa, 'The Lion King' (1994)

**90's FOREVER**

"There's no reason to have a plan B because it distracts from plan A."
- Will Smith

The 1990s was home to two summer Olympic games: the 1992 Olympics held in Barcelona, Spain, and the 1996 Olympics in Atlanta, USA. It was also home to 3 winter Olympics.

Until 1992, the Winter Olympics were held on the same year as the Summer Olympics, but in 1992, it was decided that they should be held every two years, alternating. This is why the Winter Olympics was also held two years later in 1994, and subsequently 4 years later, in 1998!

Filled with show-stopping performances, record-breaking scores, and its fair share of scandals, the Olympic Games in the 1990s has some historic moments! But how many do you remember?

1. Nancy Kerrigan won a silver medal in the 1994 Winter Olympics in Lillehammer, Norway, despite being attacked with a police club by associates of which rival figure skater?

2. In 1992, Derek Redmond was halfway through his 400m sprint representing Great Britain at the Olympics, when his hamstring snapped. Who famously helped him across the finish line?

1. Tonya Harding 2. His father

**90's TRIVIA**

## How many scandals do you remember from the 1990s Olympic Games?

3. Which legendary boxer, who was suffering from Parkinsons at the time, famously lit the Olympic Torch in Atlanta in 1996?

4. American sprinter Michael Johnson famously won a double gold for two races. But which two races did he compete? A) 100m and 200m, B) 200m and 400m, C) 200m and 800m, D) 400m and 800m

5. Which famous basketball player returned, after leaving the NBA due to a HIV diagnosis, to play in the 1992 Olympic Basketball team, dubbed 'The Dream Team'?

3. Muhammad Ali 4. B) 200m and 400m 5. Magic Johnson

Through history, something that has remained in the hearts of the world is our love of pets! However, each decade, people became obsessed with different animals to bring into their homes, with pet trends coming in and out of fashion!

In 1990, the top dog breed in the US was the cocker spaniel, which is still much loved today! However, ever since 1991, the most popular dog breed of choice has been the Labrador Retriever!

The 1990s also saw a huge popularity spike in Rottweilers, which was second place between 1992 and 1997! Recently this has dipped, which may be due to the aggressive image the Rottweiler has garnered over recent years.

German shepherds were very popular in the 1990s when compared to today, holding the third spot between 1993 until 2001! In modern days, there is far greater diversity regarding the popular dog breeds, and cross-breeding between types of dogs has resulted in an explosion of new canines in our everyday lives!

Did you own a dog growing up? If so, was it one of the more popular breeds listed above?

# 90's TRIVIA

**Are you a true canine lover? See how much you know about the most popular, and famous, dogs of the 1990s!**

1. In legally blonde, Elle Woods owns a small Chihuahua, but what was its name?

2. What small island beginning with 'N' on the Atlantic coast of Canada is reported to be the origin of the Labrador retriever?

3. In 1992, a film about a large St Bernard dog who was under threat by an evil vet was released. Which classical composer was the dog, and the film named after?

4. What's the Simpson's family dog called?

5. In 1990 and 1991, which curly-haired dog came third in the popularity rankings in the US?

1. Bruiser 2. Newfoundland 3. Beethoven 4. Santa's Little Helper 5. Poodle

**We Love The 90's**

The 90s saw many celebrities that are now household names, and trailblazers in music, cinema, television and sport — let's take a look at when some of the most famous people of the 21st century were brought into this world — thank god for the 90s (or not!)

1990: Emma Watson, Jennifer Lawrence, Kristen Stewart, Margot Robbie

1991: Ed Sheeran, Louis Tomlinson, Emma Roberts, Shailene Woodley

1992: Selena Gomez, Cardi B, Miley Cyrus, Taylor Lautner

1993: Ariana Grande, Miranda Cosgrove, Pete Davidson, Zayn Malik

1994: Justin Bieber, Harry Styles, Dakota Fanning, Halsey

1995: Kendall Jenner, Timothée Chalamet, Doja Cat, Gigi Hadid

1996: Tom Holland, Bella Hadid, Zendaya, 6IX9INE

1997: Kylie Jenner, Camila Cabello, Chloë Grace Moretz, Simone Biles

1998: Shawn Mendes, Jayden Smith, Khalid, Jack Harlow

1999: Joey King, Lily Rose Depp, Lil Nas X, Madison Beer

There is certainly a trend in celebrities born in the 90s — the younger they get, the more you may find rising stars finding their fame through internet trends and apps, as opposed to the singers and actresses born earlier in the decade — there is certainly a new era of celebrity that was about to emerge, courtesy of the 1990s!

# 90's TRIVIA

**How much do you know about some of the names listed?**

1. Kristen Stewart famously played the lead character in hit franchise, Twilight. But what was her character's full name?

2. Who are Kendall and Kylie Jenner's famous parents?

3. Harry Styles first found fame off the back of which TV show?

4. What sport does Olympian Simone Biles specialise in?

5. Which country music star featured alongside Lil Nas X in the breakout single, Old Town Road?

1. Bella Swan 2. Kris and Caitlyn Jenner 3. The X Factor 4. Gymnastics 5. Billy Ray Cyrus

Can you guess how much items used to cost back in 1990, if you are given the cost of them thirty years later, in 2020? Some might surprise you — are we paying less, or more?

### Test yourself with this fun and challenging quiz!

1. If in 2020, a loaf of bread costed on average £1.07, how much did it cost in 1990?

2. If, in 2020, 1KG Sugar is on average 75p, how much did it cost in 1990?

3. If, in 2020, 1 cucumber is 59p, how much did it cost in 1990?

4. If the average property price in 2020 was £234,000, how much was it in 1990?

5. If the average cost of a car in 2020 is around £24,000, how much was it in 1990?

1. 50p 2. 54p 3. 54p 4. £57,000 5. £12,500

**90's FOREVER**

Why not have a laugh with the other 90s babies you know with these celebrity themed jokes!

Knock knock!
Who's there?
Britney Spears.
Britney Spears who?
Knock knock!
Who's there?
Oops, I did it again!

How do you find Will Smith in the snow?
Look for the fresh prints!

Which Spice Girl can hold the most gasoline?
Geri can!

What do '90s boy bands and blue spruce trees have in common?
They all have frosted tips!

Why did David Hasselhoff change his name to "The Hoff"?
He couldn't be bothered with the hassle!

**Who says 90s kids don't have a sense of humour?! Prove them wrong with these hysterical one-liners!**

Do you know the worst part of finding yourself?
Realising you're not Waldo!

Why did scientists clone Dolly?
They wanted some sheep thrills!

What happened when the '90s kid saw a disposable camera?
It gave them a flashback!

What does Sonic the Hedgehog wear when he goes to the beach?
A speedo!

What is Forrest Gump's email password?
1Forrest1!

**Reminisce in the best decade ever with these hilarious 90s jokes!**

It was the mid 1990s, I was stuck in the desert and I thought I could see an Oasis...

But it was just a Blur.

There will be no documentation of the 1990's...
...Because only 90's kids will remember

What did the Super Nintendo say to the Sega Genesis?
"You know, everyone always tells me that I'm a BIT better than you."

What do you call part of a poem written by a Seinfeld character?
A George Co-stanza!

What do you call a grunge gardener?
Hedgy!

We Love The 90's

Much like hairdos popular amongst women of the world, male hairstyle trends also changed drastically in the 1990s, with many inspired by celebrities, popular films and TV. Some of these are even fashionable today, showing they really have stood the test of time!

Prominent through the late 1990s and early 00s, frosted tips was a popular choice for men. This involved isolating small strands of hair and bleaching them, to give the layered highlight effect! For full 90s style, these should then be spiked up with copious amounts of crunchy hair gel!

Men also started sporting a more relaxed, longer look with floppy curtains. Made popular by celebrities such as Leonardo DiCaprio and Johnny Depp, this was an easy way to try to swoon a lover! Inspired by the 90s grunge movements, and its prominent icons such as Kurt Cobain, people grew the relaxed curtain hairstyle out a little more, for a jaw-length, wavy look!

### Try your knowledge of some retro dos!

1. Which NSYNC frontman had a signature permed, frosted tips look?

2. Sported by celebrities such as George Clooney, a short-on-top and even shorter back-and-sides look was named after which Roman Emperor?

3. What popular 90s hairstyle is described as being 'business in the front, party in the back'?

1. Justin Timberlake 2. Julius Caesar 3. Mullet

We all know that one friend or family member who is convinced they are being watched. Or perhaps that the birds are spying on us? Whatever it is, conspiracy theories have dominated history, and with every great event, there is usually multiple conspiracy theories that accompany it!

Let's take a look back at some of the major conspiracy theories that were born from the 1990s!

### Ronaldo and the 1998 FIFA World Cup

In 1998, Brazil were gearing up to win the Final of the World Cup. Set to take on France, many people believed they had this in the bag! This is largely down to Brazilian player Ronaldo, who was seen as one of the world's greatest football players in history.

However, the night before the game, Ronaldo suffered an epileptic fit, which possibly led to an uncharacteristically poor performance, leading to the team's loss to France, 0-3.

The coincidental timing of this led many fans to start questioning... perhaps there is more to this story... perhaps he was drugged... who knows?

### Lizard People

Perhaps one of the more prominent and widely believed conspiracy theories of the modern day was actually started in the late 90s, courtesy of sports reporter, David Icke.

Releasing his first book called 'The Biggest Secret', Icke spoke to two Brits who believed that the Royal Family were merely lizards with crowns, sparking a huge debate into the feasibility of adult-skinned lizard people ruling the world.

This conspiracy has since spawned a massive debate into aliens and humanity, and has generational iterations, from presidents to Avril Lavigne!

### Here are three fun questions on these conspiracy theories:

1. Which major UK channel did David Icke work for, when he released his first conspiracy book?

2. How many goals were scored in total in the 1998 World Cup?
A) 73, B) 138, C) 171, D) 221

3. Which of the following were reported by Icke as being tell-tale signs that someone is a reptile?
A) Red hair and unexplained scars, B) Yellow eyes and unexplained scars, C) Red hair and yellow eyes, D) Dry skin and red hair, E) All of the above

1. BBC 2. C) 171 3. A) Red hair and unexplained scars

The 1990s saw many horror films grace our screens and scare audiences around the world – some of which have become cult classics, and legendary to many fans of the genre! But, which 90s horror film was your favourite?

One of the most iconic horror films to emerge out of 90s cinema is Scream. Released in 1996, and directed by horror legend Wes Craven (director for A Nightmare on Elm Street and The Hills Have Eyes), Scream is hailed as breathing new life into the slasher genre, playing into the stereotypes of other horror successes in the past, such as Halloween (1978) and Friday the 13th (1980).

Another successful horror/thriller film that received great critical acclaim – something that is rare for this genre of cinema – is The Silence of the Lambs. Released in 1991, this is a detective film surrounding killer cannibal Hannibal Lecter, played by Anthony Hopkins. This film actually received the prestigious 'Big Five' at the Oscars – awards for Best Picture, Best Director, Best Actor, Best Actress and Best Adapted Screenplay – impressive!

## How much do you know about 90s horror?

1. How many people died on screen in Scream?
A) 2, B) 5, C) 7, D) 10

2. How many Friday the 13th films came out in the 1990s?

3. Which film featured the iconic line – "I see dead people"

1. C) 7 2. 1 3. The Sixth Sense

## 90's TRIVIA

Every 90s kid's childhood would be incomplete without the loveable Mr Bean! Debuting in 1990, and airing 15 episodes sporadically between 1990 and 1995, Mr Bean was a character played by Rowan Atkinson, who went around seemingly mundane tasks in a wacky and unusual way, and more often than not, he found himself making more problems along the way!

Becoming a firm favourite amongst children and adults alike, Mr Bean has since inspired two feature films and has been revived in recent years in the form of a cartoon — but nothing is quite like the original!

Were you a true Mr Bean fan, or was it not a favourite in your house? Find out with the fun quiz below!

1. What kind of car does Mr Bean drive?

2. In episode 'Mr Bean in Room 426', what does he eat that makes him feel sick?

3. Which National Treasure does Mr Bean head-butt upon meeting them?

4. When he went out for dinner on his birthday, what dish does he order?

5. True or False: Mr Bean never speaks.

1. Mini Cooper 2. Oysters 3. The Queen
4. Steak Tartare 5. False!

In the 1990s, the West End, in London, saw many legendary productions hit the stage, some of which are still thriving today!

Theatre seemed to boom in the 90s, with productions becoming bigger in scale, fame and production, and audiences flocking to see productions of their favourite novels, films and musicals like never before!

1999 in particular saw two productions introduced into the West End, which quickly became favourites, and are still running today!

The first was Mamma Mia!, which debuted on the 6th April 1999. Opening at the Prince Edward theatre in the West End, this ABBA-inspired musical is the longest running jukebox musical in the history of the West End, and has been performed over 9,000 times since its opening!

Later that year, on the 19th October 1999, the on-stage adaptation of Disney's The Lion King premiered, taking the theatre world by storm! Originally starting in 1997 in Minneapolis, and famously in Broadway, New York City, the show opened in the UK at the Lyceum Theatre in the West End, where it is still performed today!

# 90's TRIVIA

**How much do you know about these two productions, both on stage and screen?**

1. What year did Disney's The Lion King come out in the 1990s – the film that is!

2. Who starred as Donna Sheridan in the film adaptation of Mamma Mia?

3. How many men are invited to Sophie's wedding, as the potential father to her in Mamma Mia!?

4. True or False – The Lion King is Broadway's highest-grossing production of all time.

5. Approximately how many performances of The Lion King have there been in the West End since its opening?
A) 6844, B) 8260, C) 9720, D) 10496

1. 1994 2. Meryl Streep 3. 3 4. True – since it's opening, it has grossed over $1 billion! 5. B

90's PARTY

We have already gone over the best-selling singles of the 1990s, but what about albums? With the 90s being the year that CDs became widely popular, album purchases were made more available and widespread, but which album came out on top?

In 1995, Oasis released (What's the Story) Morning Glory? — This went on to be the biggest-selling album of the 1990s. It sold a record-breaking 345,000 copies in its first week in the UK, and spent a whopping 10 weeks at number 1 on the UK Albums Chart! Featuring some of the band's most famous hits, including 'Some Might Say', 'Don't Look Back in Anger', and 'Wonderwall', it's no surprise that this album was so popular!

## The top 10 biggest selling albums of the decade were:

1. (What's the Story) Morning Glory? - Oasis
2. Stars - Simply Red
3. Spice - Spice Girls
4. Talk on Corners - The Corrs
5. Jagged Little Pill - Alanis Morissette
6. Robson & Jerome - Robson & Jerome
7. The Immaculate Collection - Madonna
8. Urban Hymns - The Verve
9. Gold: Greatest Hits - ABBA
10. Falling into You - Celine Dion

# NINETIES IN OUR HEARTS

How much do you know about the biggest selling albums of the nineties, and the artists who released them?

1. What country are The Corrs from?

2. What was the lead single from The Verve's Urban Hymns, which is now seen as their signature song?

3. 10th on the track listing for Alanis Morissette is her well-known hit, Ironic. What did she say would be ironic if it happened on your wedding day?

4. Which of the above albums in the top 10 is the longest in length?

5. How many studio albums did Oasis release?

1. Ireland 2. Bittersweet Symphony 3. Rain
4. Gold: Greatest Hits – ABBA 5. 7

The 90s had its fair share of scandals, involving respected celebrities, royals and politicians all around the world! As much as times have changed since the nineties, the public still love a scandal! Let's look at two of the most news-dominating and decade-defining moments of the 1990s!

### Bill Clinton and Monica Lewinsky

US president Bill Clinton was the leader of the Democratic Party, and held office in the US between 1993 and 2001. However, during his presidency, the president admitted to having an affair with White House intern Monica Lewinsky. These relations were reported to have taken place between 1995 and 1996, and the scandal is both rooted in his infidelity to wife, Hillary Clinton, and whether or not he lied under oath about his behaviour.

This scandal ultimately resulted in Bill Clinton's impeachment in 1999, making him the second president ever to be impeached whilst in office. Since this time, Lewinsky's name has reportedly been mentioned in over 100 rap songs. And let's not forget her infamous stained blue dress...

## Hugh Grant and Elizabeth Hurley

Ah yes... Hugh Grant, the dishy actor that, in the 1990s, had the world's heart. Seen as somewhat an innocent English gentleman, supported by his character representations in 90s films such as Four Weddings and a Funeral, his behaviour in 1995 sent shockwaves across his fan base.

He was arrested by LAPD after paying a sex worker, Divine Brown, $60 for lewd acts. This shattered the image people had of the English actor, but surprisingly didn't end their relationship!

Elizabeth Hurley stuck by his side through the scandal, and despite this tumultuous time, they continued to date, until they ended amicably in 2000.

Actress and Model Elizabeth Hurley also maintains a sense of humour throughout the whole ordeal, and on her show 'The Royals', the character she played hired an escort, whose name was 'Huge Grant'... It's a shame the rest of the world took things a little more seriously!

# THE 90's

MANY MEMORIES.

NO EVIDENCE.